READING GALATIANS

CASCADE COMPANIONS

The Christian theological tradition provides an embarrassment of riches: from Scripture to modern scholarship, we are blessed with a vast and complex theological inheritance. And yet this feast of traditional riches is too frequently inaccessible to the general reader.

The Cascade Companions series addresses the challenge by publishing books that combine academic rigor with broad appeal and readability. They aim to introduce nonspecialist readers to that vital storehouse of authors, documents, themes, histories, arguments, and movements that comprise this heritage with brief yet compelling volumes.

RECENT TITLES IN THIS SERIES:

Cascade Companion to Evil by Charles Taliaferro
Metaphysics by Donald Wallenfang
Phenomenology by Donald Wallenfang
Virtue by Olli-Pekka Vainio
Reading Paul by Michael Gorman
The Rule of Faith by Everett Ferguson
The Second-Century Apologists by Alvyn Pettersen
Origen by Ronald E. Heine
Athanasius of Alexandria by Lois Farag
Practicing Lament by Rebekah Eklund
Forgiveness: A Theology by Anthony Bash
Called to Attraction: The Theology of Beauty by Brendan T. Sammon
A Primer in Ecotheology by Celia Deane-Drummond
Postmodern Theology by Carl Raschke
Jacques Ellul by Jacob E. Van Vleet and Jacob M. Rollinson
Understanding Pannenberg by Anthony C. Thiselton
The Becoming of God: Process Theology by Ronald Faber
Theology and Science Fiction by James F. McGrath
The U.S. Immigration Crisis by Miguel de la Torre
Feminism and Christianity by Caryn Riswold
Queer Theology by Linn Marie Tonstad

READING GALATIANS

JOHN ANTHONY DUNNE

CASCADE *Books* • Eugene, Oregon

READING GALATIANS

Copyright © 2025 John Anthony Dunne. All rights reserved. Except for brief quotations in critical publications or reviews, no part of this book may be reproduced in any Wipf and Stock Publishers, 199 W. 8th Ave., Suite 3, Eugene, OR 97401.

Cascade Books
An Imprint of Wipf and Stock Publishers
199 W. 8th Ave., Suite 3
Eugene, OR 97401

www.wipfandstock.com

PAPERBACK ISBN: 978-1-6667-3842-1
HARDCOVER ISBN: 978-1-6667-9909-5
EBOOK ISBN: 978-1-6667-9910-1

Cataloguing-in-Publication data:

Names: Dunne, John Anthony, author.

Title: Reading Galatians / John Anthony Dunne.

Description: Eugene, OR: Cascade Books, 2025. | Cascade Companions. | Includes bibliographical references and index.

Identifiers: ISBN 978-1-6667-3842-1 (paperback). | ISBN 978-1-6667-9909-5 (hardcover). | ISBN 978-1-6667-9910-1 (ebook).

Subjects: LCSH: Bible. Galatians—Criticism, interpretation, etc. | Bible. N.T.—Epistles of Paul—Criticism, interpretation, etc.

Classification: BS2685.52 D866 2025 (print). | BS2685.52 (ebook).

VERSION NUMBER 05/12/25

Scripture quotations are taken from the New Revised Standard Version Updated Edition. Copyright © 2021 National Council of Churches of Christ in the United States of America. Used by permission. All rights reserved worldwide.

For Chris Spinks

CONTENTS

Preface and Introduction | ix

1 Galatians as a Peculiar Letter | 1

2 Strategies for Reading Galatians | 18

3 Paul's Initial Visit to Galatia | 38

4 After Paul Left Galatia | 61

5 Paul's Response to the Galatians, Part One: Paul Is a Paradigm for Galatian Imitation | 83

6 Paul's Response to the Galatians, Part Two: The Law Protected the Promise to Abraham | 94

7 Paul's Response to the Galatians, Part Three: Those with the Spirit are Above the Law | 109

8 What Did the Galatians Do with Paul's Letter? | 126

9 What Do We Do with Paul's Letter to the Galatians? | 139

Bibliography | 149

Name Index | 157

Subject Index | 159

Ancient Documents Index | 161

PREFACE AND INTRODUCTION

ACADEMIA IS STRUCTURED so that academics stay in their respective lanes. Although I am an academic, I am not one for lanes. Sure, I do have a lane (or two), but venturing out beyond it is what propels me forward once I get back in it. This is because, unlike cats, curiosity is what gives me life, and I am curious about way too many things. Nevertheless, Galatians has been the center of gravity constantly tugging at me as I indulge my eclectic interests in the broader universe of biblical studies. As an Enneagram 7 with ADHD and an insatiable desire to learn, it is very easy for me to get distracted and to want to study something new. But Galatians has always had a way of keeping me in its orbit. I continue to return to it after ventures in other galaxies of thought, and each time I am reminded anew that I have arrived at a place both wonderful and strange. With this book, *Reading Galatians*, it thrills me to provide you, dear reader, with something of a guide for exploring Galatians on your own—one that builds upon and condenses some of the insights that I have gleaned from my previous outings into the wild world of Paul's most untamed letter.

As a way of providing a map for this journey, we begin by highlighting what makes Galatians unique and defamiliarizing ourselves from what we might think we know about the letter in chapter 1. Then in chapter 2, I survey the landscape of previous interpretation of the letter, noting how other scholars and theologians have read Galatians with beneficial results, and what trends characterize those ways of reading it. Chapters 3–4 then take a chronological approach to investigating the crisis in Galatia. I begin in chapter 3 by asking what we can learn about Paul's initial ministry to Galatia from the letter itself, and bring that into conversation with the record of Paul's missionary journeys in Acts. Chapter 4 explores what we can uncover about what transpired in Paul's absence after he left Galatia, which gave way to the crisis. Then chapters 5–7 are my attempt to highlight three key features from Paul's response to the Galatians regarding the crisis that emerged. Chapter 8, after that, reflects on what we can glean from the letter itself about how the Galatians may have responded, before turning to other potential bits of evidence about whether Paul's letter was a success in his day. Finally, in chapter 9, I finish off the book by considering how Paul's ancient letter relates to contemporary readers today. And just so you know, throughout the book, all translations of biblical languages are my own, except where I indicate otherwise. My hope is that by offering this type of an overview of Galatians in the present book it will open up new avenues and connections than previously noticed. Along the way I not only try to point out areas of concern for anyone reading Galatians, but I also do so by offering *a reading of Galatians*, which I hope you will find both engaging and compelling.

The entire team at Wipf and Stock are due my deep thanks for giving me the opportunity to contribute to the Cascade Companions series. In particular, I am indebted to Chris Spinks for taking on the project after chatting about the idea with me in the bookstalls of the annual SBL meeting in San Antonio in 2021. Sadly, Chris passed away in Spring 2024 from brain cancer, and so I did not get to work with him as an editor, which I deeply regret. Since this book would not exist without him, I dedicate it to his memory. May he rest peacefully, rise powerfully, and reign perpetually.

When Chris first signed me up for *Reading Galatians*, he told me to write it as if I was teaching an informed Adult Sunday School class. That advice was spot on, and it prompted me to teach through the book as an actual Adult Sunday School class. Although Salem Covenant Church in New Brighton, Minnesota, is not my home church, I taught a course on Galatians there like I have done many times on other topics ever since I moved to Minnesota. I have never come across a more organized, engaged, and invested Adult Sunday School class, and it is always such a joy to teach there. Even though a class on Galatians doesn't sound like it would offer the same level of excitement as the classes I taught for them in the past on topics like *Harry Potter* (2019) and wine in the Bible (2022), they were just as eager to learn—and since "sorcery" and "drunkenness" are mentioned in Gal 5:19–21, I reminded them that we remained on target! I wish to thank them for continuing to invite me back, and for being the guinea pigs for this book.

For anything that I do on Galatians it must be said that I owe so much gratitude to Professor N. T. Wright, who was my doctoral supervisor at the University of St Andrews when I first started working on Galatians. I remain deeply appreciative of his advice, insight, correction, encouragement, and friendship since 2011, which informs and suffuses the present book. The same goes for my *Doktorbruder*, J. Andrew Cowan (who gave extensive feedback on an early draft), and also my *Galaterbruder* from another *Doktorvater*, Logan Williams, who both are always great sounding boards for various musings on Paul and Galatians.

Several people read through drafts or partial drafts of this book, and offered invaluable feedback. Special thanks to Nick Fox, Ryan Heinsch, Dustin Thompson, and Justin Winzenburg for reading the full draft and joining me for a proper symposium to discuss the book, and also to Luke and Emalea Beavers for reading a draft and conversing with me about some key points on a couple of occasions. I am also grateful to my former student, Micah Carpenter, and a few of my Greek Exegesis students at Bethel Seminary, who were willing to take on an extra assignment of reading and commenting on a draft of this book as we translated through the Greek text of Galatians for class, particularly Michael Beltz, Robert Berg, and Esa Hytti, as well as my TA, Billy Hinshaw. All of the input that I received contributed to the present form of the book, so thanks to everyone for helping to make it better!

Lastly, I am grateful to my family, by blood and by faith—my parents, my siblings and their spouses, and my nieces, Isla Belle, Calli Christine, and Layla Rae, and my nephew, Jacob Thomas. I hope you all grasp what Paul says when he affirms that nothing else matters when compared to the kind of faith that walks around in the real world looking like love.

John Anthony Dunne
Pentecost 2024

1

GALATIANS AS A PECULIAR LETTER

Paul's letter to the Galatians is so often treated as familiar territory. It is Paul's treatise on freedom, some will say.[1] For plenty of others it is a repository of discrete passages ready when you need them, like a biblical Room of Requirement from *Harry Potter*, within which armchair theologians and theobros find ammunition for debates about justification, and Bible study leaders find a quick lesson on the fruit of the Spirit. But whether we reduce all of Galatians to a single concept, or mine it for single passages, we are casually assuming that we have tamed what is utterly wild.

I've always thought that Galatians is one of the more peculiar letters of Paul. At first blush, that might sound odd. Galatians is often regarded as a miniature version of Romans—a fiery first draft before cooler heads prevailed.

1. E.g., Peterson, *Traveling Light*.

Yet, despite some superficial overlap with Romans, including how both texts talk about justification by faith and appeal to the example of Abraham, Galatians does a number of things that no other Pauline letter does. But what exactly should we expect from a Pauline letter?

GALATIANS COMPARED TO OTHER LETTERS

Ancient letters tended to follow the same broad outline.[2] They begin by naming the author(s) and the recipient(s) of the letter, often including a warm greeting of some kind. Then the author(s) typically shifts to offer a word of thanks for the recipient(s). After these pleasantries comes the heart of things, what we call the body of the letter. The different lengths of letters typically come down to the length of the body. Philemon is the shortest of Paul's letters, with the shortest body among them (verses 8–22), although it is closer in size to the average length of an ancient letter. So Philemon might be an aberration for Paul, but that's only because Paul's letters are an aberration among ancient letters. After the letter's body comes the final section, called the letter closing, in which the author(s) briefly signs off and typically adds a final prayer or blessing for the original audience. Galatians more or less follows this same outline, but with some notable tweaks that, again, make it stand out as a unique Pauline letter.

To start, when Paul identifies himself as the author (or an author) of one of his letters, he typically designates himself as an "apostle" (1 Cor 1:1; 2 Cor 1:1; Eph 1:1; Col 1:1; 1 Tim 1:1; 2 Tim 1:1), or "slave" (Phil 1:1), or both (Rom 1:1; Tit 1:1). On one occasion he identifies himself

---

2. For helpful studies on Paul and ancient letter writing, see, e.g., Richards, *Paul and First-Century Letter-Writing*; Weima, *Paul the Ancient Letter Writer*.

as a "prisoner" (Phlm 1), and when writing to the Thessalonians he uses no titles at all (1 Thess 1:1; 2 Thess 1:1). Galatians fits the broader pattern, where Paul does provide a self-designation—here it's "apostle" as with most others (Gal 1:1)—but unlike his other letters, Paul immediately proceeds to defend or qualify his title of "apostle," which we do not see elsewhere.[3] Look at how Paul begins his letter:

> **Gal 1:1:** Paul, an apostle, not from people, nor through a person, but through Jesus Christ and God the Father, who raised him from the dead.

Paul then goes on to name co-senders, but unlike Timothy, Silas, or Sosthenes, whom Paul names elsewhere (1 Cor 1:1; 2 Cor 1:1; Phil 1:1; Col 1:1; 1 Thess 1:1; 2 Thess 1:1; Phlm 1), here Paul's co-senders are a host of unnamed people—"all the siblings who are with me" (Gal 1:2).

The Galatians are obviously the recipients of the letter, but when Paul mentions them there are a couple of notable things to mention. For one, his recipients include multiple churches spread out across a Roman province, whereas elsewhere he addresses a single city (Romans; 1–2 Corinthians; Philippians; 1–2 Thessalonians; Colossians; Ephesians), an individual (1–2 Timothy; Titus) or a household (Philemon).[4] The Galatians are also not given any flowery description like Paul gives his audience in other letters. Paul simply writes, "to the churches of Galatia" (Gal 1:2). Elsewhere Paul addresses the Romans as "beloved of God in Rome, called to be saints" (Rom 1:7), the Corinthians as part of "the church of God, which is in Corinth, sanctified

---

3. Aside from the possible exception in 2 Cor 1:1: "an apostle of Christ Jesus *by the will of God.*"

4. Two exceptions to this are that 2 Corinthians is addressed to Corinth and "the whole of Achaia" (2 Cor 1:1), and Ephesians may have been a circular letter written to southwestern Asia Minor since some early manuscripts don't mention Ephesus in the opening verse.

by Christ Jesus, called to be saints" (1 Cor 1:2), and the Philippians as "all the holy ones in Christ Jesus who are in Philippi with the overseers and deacons" (Phil 1:1). Indeed, every other letter bearing Paul's name contains some type of positive affirmation of the recipients, just not this one.

These changes so far reflect divergence in *Pauline* style, where Paul does something different compared to his other letters, but he also adjusts the standard practice from how other people often wrote letters in the ancient world as well. Most notably, when Paul finishes the initial greeting, he offers no thanksgiving on behalf of the Galatians, as he does elsewhere in keeping with the convention of letter-writing. For comparison, note how the thanksgiving in Philemon begins:

> **Phlm 4–5a:** I thank my God always as I remember you in my prayers, because I hear of your love and faith . . .

In Galatians, by contrast, Paul jumps straight in after the initial greeting with an ironic rebuke (Gal 1:6–9).

> **Gal 1:6:** I marvel that you are turning so quickly from the one who called you in the grace of Christ to another gospel.

Paul's "marvel" is ironic because it is as if he is complimenting the Galatians for how much they are getting it wrong.[5] We might imagine someone offering a sarcastic and patronizing comment like this today: "Good job, guys, you're doing a fine job of screwing things up!"

Letters do not have to cohere with a standardized pattern in order to be a letter. Authors can freely deploy and

---

5. Nanos, *Irony of Galatians*, rightly highlights the irony here, and elsewhere.

adapt literary conventions.[6] But the deviation from normal practice here in Galatians likely indicates something. As we will see, in a letter in which Paul calls his readers "foolish" and "bewitched" (Gal 3:1, 3)—which are also unparalleled in Paul!—we should not be too surprised that he fails to say anything nice about them up front or offer a thanksgiving to God for them. Might this also explain the other unique features, such as Paul defending or qualifying his title as "apostle," or naming lots of fellow siblings in the faith as co-senders?

What seems to support a positive answer to those questions is how the letter proceeds after the rebuke section. Paul offers an extended autobiographical narrative about his initial calling and his subsequent ministry and interactions with the apostles in Jerusalem (Gal 1:10—2:21). Nowhere else in his letters does Paul narrate this history, although he alludes to his initial persecuting activity against the church (cf. Phil 3:6; 1 Tim 1:15) and his transformative encounter with Christ elsewhere (cf. 2 Cor 4:4). Why does Paul see the need to offer all of this information? Is it being contested or narrated differently to the Galatians? Or might the events that Paul narrates from his life provide an example for the Galatians to follow in their present setting? And could it possibly be a bit of both? Regardless of what the answer is, only here in Galatians does Paul swear an oath about what he narrates, declaring emphatically that he is not lying about any of it (Gal 1:20). Why the need to insist so strongly in the story he is telling?

Within the body of the letter, Paul makes particular hermeneutical moves and talks about certain topics that he does not mention elsewhere. For example, Galatians is the only place where you'll find Paul talk about the much-loved

---

6. For more on the way that genres are adaptable, rather than rigid, see Judd, *Modern Genre Theory*.

fruit of the Spirit (Gal 5:22–23), and the same applies to other things like "the Israel of God" (Gal 6:16), or "the marks of Jesus" (Gal 6:17). Nowhere else does Paul call Jesus "the seed of Abraham" (Gal 3:16), nor does he ever refer to the fact that Jesus was born of a woman and born under the law (Gal 4:4). It is only in Galatians that Paul conceives of the law as a temporary guardian (Gal 3:24), something secondary to God's purposes with Abraham (Gal 3:15–18), which also places a curse on those who fail to keep it (Gal 3:10). Galatians is also the only letter of Paul that overtly articulates that scripture can have an allegorical meaning (Gal 4:21—5:1).[7] To be sure, he does say in 1 Corinthians 9 that legislation about not muzzling oxen while they tread grain addresses compensation for ministry (1 Cor 9:9; cf. Deut 25:4). Yet such an interpretation is small-minded stuff compared to the convoluted argument that he offers in Galatians, something that meme-culture nowadays would label as "galaxy brain."

Finally, Paul also finishes his letter to the Galatians in a very unique way. As Paul brings the body of the letter to an end (Gal 6:11–17), just before the official closing of the letter (Gal 6:18),[8] he draws attention to his handwriting.[9]

> **Gal 6:11:** See with what large letters I wrote to you by my hand.

Nowhere else does Paul make this kind of fuss about his handwriting. To be sure, he comments on the fact that he writes parts of his letters by hand (Col 4:18; 2 Thess 3:17; Phlm 19), but nowhere does he remark on what his

---

7. Or, if Thiessen is correct, that the Abraham story is itself an allegory (*Jewish Paul*, 95).

8. See Hubing, *Crucifixion and New Creation*.

9. Cf. writing in large letters in Plutarch, *Cato Major* 20:4–5 (348), as cited in Elder, *Gospel Media*, 138.

handwriting actually looks like. At times, Paul authored or co-authored his letters by dictation, which meant that a scribe was responsible for putting pen to paper, so to speak, or stylus to papyrus, as the case may have been. In the case of Romans, we know the scribe was named Tertius (Rom 16:22). Whether Tertius was responsible for any other letters, we cannot say, but it is likely that scribes worked with Paul more than just the once. So when Paul refers to his own handwriting, it probably does not mean that he wrote the entirety of those letters by hand, but rather simply the final greeting. This would add a nice personal touch, convey authenticity, and signify his approval of what was written.

The exception here is probably Philemon, as argued by Nicholas Elder, because of its short length and personal nature, and also because Paul's reference to his handwriting appears before the closing of the letter and instead is found within the body itself (Phlm 19).[10] In Galatians as well, Paul's acknowledgement of his own handwriting occurs at the end of the body of the letter, albeit at the end of a much longer body than Philemon. Does this suggest that Paul wrote all of Galatians by hand? My inclination on this is that Paul takes "pen in hand" for Gal 6:11 through to the official letter closing in 6:18, rather than for the full letter, because he wants to personalize the end of his argument and draw attention to his summary comments about what is at stake in Galatia. If we were to look at the outgoing copy of the letter, then, we'd presumably see a noticeable shift in penmanship as the text moved from the scribal hand to Paul's large letters.

But why has Paul written with such large letters? It has been suggested that Paul writes this way because of factors he couldn't control, such as having rough hands from working as a tent-maker (cf. 1 Thess 2:9; 2 Thess 3:7–8; Acts

10. Elder, "This Hand Is Validation."

18:2–3) or from potentially having poor eye sight (*ophthalmia*; cf. Gal 4:15). It's more likely that Paul draws attention to his handwriting because of something he was doing on purpose for emphasis. A modern example would be using bold face type or writing in "ALL CAPS." In other words, it seems that Paul wants to make sure that if they don't remember anything else, they make sure to remember what he's about to say in what follows. As Hans Dieter Betz has remarked, Gal 6:11–17 then functions as a "hermeneutical key" for interpreting the rest of the letter,[11] which I think is exactly right, and we will return to it to help us unlock more than one tricky part of the letter.

WHY THE PECULIARITY OF GALATIANS MATTERS

What do all of these distinctive features tell us about Galatians? Together they might serve to indicate something about the unique situation that Paul is addressing as well as the kind of emotional state he may have been in while writing Galatians, which brings us to a very important point about interpreting any letter like this from antiquity.

Since letters are written to particular people, we have to remember that we're reading someone else's mail. Letters give us insight into the correspondence between ancient people, but they only give us one side of that conversation. We don't know what we're missing from the communication, making it sort of like overhearing one side of a phone call. The distinctive features of Galatians also remind us that letters are *occasional*, meaning that they arise from a specific set of circumstances (i.e., a specific *occasion*). Paul sends letters as a pastor and missionary, addressing concerns as they arise in the communities he founded in an *ad*

---

11. Betz, *Galatians*, 313.

hoc manner.[12] As real-life issues present themselves, Paul deploys scripture and theological insight for practical purposes. Not one of his letters is actually a theological treatise on a subject. What Paul says to the Galatians is meant to address the problems arising in Galatia, and so he's not necessarily going to address the same things to Jesus followers in Philippi or Thessalonica or anywhere else, even Rome, because the situation is different. Paul also wrote his letters over the course of a multi-decade ministry, and so things changed and developed, not least Paul himself.

Paul also sends letters because he cannot be there in person to address the matter firsthand. His letters then function as his surrogate in his absence. He even hints at this at one point:

> **Gal 4:20:** I would like to be present with you now and change my tone, because I am perplexed by you.

Paul here admits his frustration, and acknowledges that his tone would be different if he were with them. As we all know from texting and emails, it is notoriously difficult to tell tone with written speech, but in a letter where Paul calls his readers "foolish," we could have guessed that Paul wasn't very happy without him confirming it explicitly.

And if it wasn't clear, Paul will go on to express such deep frustration with a shadowy group causing trouble in Galatia, of whom he says he wishes that they would castrate themselves (Gal 5:12). Now, I don't know about you, but I have never wished such a thing on anyone, and I'm sure I'd have to be pretty ticked off to even entertain the thought, so the circumstances in Galatia, again, have made Paul furious. And uniquely so, because he doesn't talk like this in

---

12. Cf. Bird and Dunne, "Pastoring with a Big Stick."

any of his other letters. Once more, Galatians is a peculiar letter.

IS GALATIANS TOO PECULIAR?

Galatians is perhaps such an outlier that it is surprising that more scholars do not doubt whether Paul even wrote it. Scholars debate the Pauline authorship of six letters attributed to Paul. These are the so-called "disputed letters," which are Colossians, Ephesians, 2 Thessalonians, 1–2 Timothy, and Titus, but Galatians has never been seriously questioned. It belongs to the scholarly construct of the "undisputed letters," which are taken as authentic. These include Romans, 1–2 Corinthians, Galatians, Philippians, 1 Thessalonians, and Philemon. The reason for scholarly doubt of the "disputed letters" is because of a combination of factors that include differences in style, terminology, theological emphases, ecclesial organization, and eschatological expectation.

But before the "undisputed letters" were solidified as such, F. C. Baur, a 19th century German New Testament scholar based at the University of Tübingen, argued that only four letters could be certainly attributed to Paul. These are known as the "Head Letters" (or the *Hauptbriefe* in German), which include the first four letters of the Pauline collection in our printed Bibles: Romans, 1–2 Corinthians, and Galatians.[13] The list of seven undisputed letters is simply an extension of these four. Because of its history as being among the "Head Letters" and now among the "undisputed letters," Galatians goes virtually unquestioned. But as we have seen, viewing Galatians as characteristically Pauline is at least somewhat humorous.

---

13. We should not think that the placement of Galatians as fourth in the list reduces its significance. See Landgraf, "A Cinderella Story."

Years ago, Harold Hoehner wrote an article about how different Galatians is among the Pauline collection, and in a tongue-in-cheek manner, he argued that if the criteria used to question Pauline authorship was applied to Galatians, we'd have to doubt its authenticity as well.[14] I have no intention of making the same point Hoehner did, but I do share the viewpoint that Galatians is actually fairly strange. And when we factor in that (a) we have a small sample size of Paul's writings, (b) ancient letters were written for different occasions, (c) circumstances can change as well as the author, (d) Paul variously composed letters by hand and by dictation, and (e) composition included collaboration with different co-authors and/or scribes, then much of the weight behind the scholarly doubt of the disputed letters goes away. Those letters become just as *consistently inconsistent* within the Pauline letter collection as Galatians.

WHAT IS PAUL ADDRESSING AND HOW DOES HE ADDRESS IT IN GALATIANS?

If Galatians is an occasional letter, then, to what situation does it respond? When we read through the letter as a whole (which is how any letter should be read), rather than selectively engage with portions of it, it becomes clear that the entire letter addresses a single question: do the males among the gentile believers in Christ need to receive circumcision (i.e., the removal of the foreskin that covers the glans of the penis)? This is something that becomes crystal clear by the end of the letter (cf. Gal 5:2–6; 6:12–16), but that does not mean that Paul is building up to the topic. Additionally, as we will see, there is more to say about what is causing these grown men to want to undergo this procedure.

14. Hoehner, "Did Paul Write Galatians?"

What then is Paul *doing* with his letter as he addresses the male circumcision of gentiles? One scholar, Hans Dieter Betz, argued that the ancient rhetorical handbooks provide the best entry point here since they provide instructions on how to be most rhetorically effective. The best way to give speeches is to deploy one of three genres. These are the following:

1. Juridical rhetoric argues in defense of something.
2. Deliberative rhetoric aims to persuade an audience about what to do or not do.
3. Epideictic rhetoric offers praise for something.

With these categories in mind, could it be that Galatians is Paul's defense of himself, the legitimacy of his apostleship to the gentiles, and the truthfulness of his law-free gospel, and so be an example of *juridical rhetoric*, as Betz argued?[15] Or, is Galatians written primarily to persuade his gentile audience not to receive circumcision, making it *deliberative rhetoric* instead?[16] Scholars found themselves primarily drawn to one of these two camps, but then some wondered why it couldn't be a bit of both. Maybe Paul is defending himself *and* trying to persuade the Galatians not to get circumcised. So then the letter could be seen as mixing juridical in the first half with deliberative in the second half.[17] Yet I would contend that the reason that Galatians does not seem to neatly fit either of these categories is because ancient rhetoric *was intended for speeches*, not letters.[18]

With all of the letter's bells and whistles, Paul's argument essentially boils down to the fact that the Galatians

15. Betz, "Literary Composition and Function."
16. E.g., Kennedy, *New Testament Interpretation*, 145.
17. E.g., Longenecker, *Galatians*, c–cxix.
18. See esp. Kern, *Rhetoric and Galatians*.

do not need to receive circumcision in the midst of this conflict and indeed they should not. But this singular purpose is not due to the fact that Galatians is, in the end, deliberative rhetoric. Paul at times appears to be defending himself and his gospel, and he deploys many different types of arguments along the way, appealing to scripture and the experiences of the Galatians to make his case.

OUTLINING GALATIANS

So then, from a 30,000-foot perspective, how does the letter of Galatians unfold as Paul seeks to address circumcision and make his argument? Building upon the classic structure of an ancient letter that we have already seen, we can break down Galatians like this:

- Gal 1:1–5: The Initial Greeting
- Gal 1:6–9: An Ironic Rebuke
- Gal 1:10—6:17: The Body of the Letter
- Gal 6:18: The Letter Closing

As you can see, I've identified that the Body of the Letter is quite long. Some scholars regard all of Gal 6:11–18 to be the letter closing, but it seems best to view verse 18 as the actual closing to the letter. We can sub-divide the Body of the Letter further in what I prefer to see as three broad movements:

- Gal 1:10—2:21: The Autobiography
- Gal 3:1—6:10: The Heart of the Argument from Scripture and the Experience of the Spirit
- Gal 6:11–17: The Closing of the Body of the Letter

Of course, this could be sub-divided further, but I don't find it terribly helpful to do so. Galatians 1:10 is notoriously hard to place; does it belong with the ironic rebuke or is it the beginning of the autobiography? Scholars go back and forth on this, but I tend to view the questions about persuading people and people pleasing to set up the autobiography. Following from the autobiography, Gal 3:1—6:10 is admittedly a large stretch, and it does have several discrete units, but what subdividing this section further often does is obscure the fact that *Paul is still arguing*.[19] He does not shift somewhere within there to a separate ethical exhortation, as is so often assumed, including by those that believed that Galatians moves from juridical to deliberative rhetoric.

At least since the writings of Rudolf Bultmann, a prominent twentieth-century German NT scholar, it has been common to think of biblical letters as containing two broad sections which move from the so-called "indicative" to the so-called "imperative." In other words, according to this scheme, the first half of a biblical letter affirms its readers in the theological truths that apply to them, and then only after establishing the identity of the reader and the reality of who they already are, does the letter shift to the imperatives, the commands about how to live consistent with that identity and reality. In short, we could say that the first half of a letter provides theology and the second half provides the ethics. This is a common grid for reading biblical letters and it has been applied to Galatians as well.

Those who hold to this grid have wondered where exactly the ethical section of the letter begins, and so scholars looked at key imperatives around the midway point for clues (e.g., those in Gal 4:12; 4:30; and 5:1). In the early twentieth century, some scholars actually couldn't understand how

---

19. Though see, rightly, Matera, "Culmination of Paul's Argument."

Galatians as a Peculiar Letter

Paul would address ethical matters in Galatians given his opposition to "works of the law." It was even suggested that maybe Paul had to fight on two fronts: some in Galatia were becoming legalists, and others were becoming libertines. In other words, Paul had to argue against those observing the law too strictly and rigidly, and those discarding any kind of law whatsoever. But such a breakdown, for both the letter and the audience of the letter, has been rightly rejected. Yet even though scholars didn't want to say that Paul was fighting on two fronts, they still wanted, in effect, to understand the letter as having two broad movements along the lines of the indicative and the imperative. This whole conversation is rather silly to me, though, if I'm honest. It assumes that we cannot have imperatives in an indicative section and vice versa.

It reminds me of an (admittedly absurd) example from the cartoon *Family Guy* (S4.E14 from 2005). The scene I have in mind depicts the (fictional) origin of *Reese's Peanut Butter Cups*. The comedic origin story is that two drunk drivers crash into each other head on. One driver, having consumed plenty of beer, enjoys a chocolate bar, and the other one, likewise shifting away from beer, enjoys a jar of peanut butter. At the moment of the crash, the one man's chocolate bar went in to the other man's peanut butter jar. When "Officer Reese's" arrives on the scene to investigate the accident, the only thing that the two drivers could think to say in the moment is "he got peanut butter on my chocolate" and "he got chocolate in my peanut butter."

I contend, therefore, that Galatians does not have a discrete "ethical section." Ethics and argumentation suffuse the whole body of the letter. This means, for example, that when we read about the fruit of the Spirit in Galatians 5, we cannot abstract what Paul says there as a disconnected reflection floating on its own without any context rather than the chevron pattern it's printed on (which, let's be honest, is so often what happens). Rather, the fruit of the Spirit is part of an argument—indeed, an argument about why the gentile men in Galatia should not receive circumcision.

WHY DOES PAUL CARE SO MUCH?

Paul does not want these gentile men to be circumcised. Got it. But like . . . why? Moreover, why is he so fired up about it? Does all of this talk about male anatomy make Galatians hopelessly androcentric and indeed phallocentric? To be fair, Galatians often inspires the kind of humor that guys tend to enjoy. I think of a particular meme that someone once created, which might just be the best biblical studies meme I've ever seen. Perhaps you know it already. It's the meme of an angry Pakistani cricket fan, named Mohammad Sarim Akhtar, looking on to a match disapprovingly with his hands on his hips in disbelief, and the caption above him says, "The guy at the church in Galatia who was circumcised the day before Paul's letter arrived." It's brilliant. And if you have never seen it before, please do yourself a favor and Google it. On a similar note, I once received an undergraduate student paper on Galatians, from a student who shall remain nameless, that actually contained the following sentence in the concluding paragraph: "Paul, therefore, was called to preach to the genitals that they do not need to be circumcised." The mistake here is particularly funny because it makes great grammatical sense in English, and because misspelling gentile with genital (which spell-check would not flag) can perhaps be forgiven as a legitimate Freudian slip considering what Paul directly addresses in the letter. But what is it about circumcision that matters so much? Is it a proxy for some other concern? Or are there other factors that make circumcision uniquely disconcerting in this conflict? This is where it will be helpful to identify some of the major trends in the interpretation of Galatians, which are the focus of the next chapter.

REFLECTIONS

1. What do you make of all of the unique features of Galatians, and how might they affect how you approach reading the letter?
2. Why do you think Paul is so upset about gentile circumcision?

2

STRATEGIES FOR READING GALATIANS

Throughout church history, Galatians has been read in a handful of different ways, but it has undoubtedly been in the last century that the greatest number of new and innovative approaches has emerged. Some of these are worth identifying in this chapter, since their proponents will be dialogue partners at key points in the rest of the book, even if only implicitly so. I refer to these distinct approaches to Galatians as reading strategies. Each of them, in their own ways, highlight key elements of the letter and try to offer a coherent picture of what Paul seems to be saying in order to read Galatians profitably. The six strategies that we should be familiar with moving forward are the following:

1. Patristic & Medieval Readings
2. Lutheran/Reformational Readings
3. New Perspective Readings

4. Apocalyptic Readings
5. Counter-Imperial Readings
6. Paul within Judaism Readings

In this chapter I will unfortunately need *to paint with far too broad of a brush* as I aim to create a brief portrait of what each of these reading strategies are all about. My focus will be on highlighting some of the distinctives that are central to each of them, without delving too much into the many ways that people have nuanced these perspectives in their own ways. I will also address a unifying topic from Galatians as the way to get straight to the heart of things, which is the nature of the crisis in Galatia regarding circumcision, and how that pertains to Paul's understanding of "works of the law."

1. PATRISTIC & MEDIEVAL READINGS

The patristic and medieval eras both cover huge swaths of time in which different traditions and emphases on reading Scripture emerged.[1] Treating these eras in isolation, let alone together, is admittedly reductionistic. The patristic era covers the time of the church fathers in the first few centuries of the church in antiquity and late antiquity until the late fifth century CE. The medieval era then spans onward from there through to the start of the Reformation in the sixteenth century CE. So again, if we're going to paint over 1,500 years of interpretation in this brief survey, then, to paraphrase the film, *JAWS*, we're gonna need a bigger brush!

One of the reasons why pulling patristic and medieval interpreters together makes sense, however, is because of

---

1. E.g., Levy, *Letter to the Galatians*; Riches, *Galatians Through the Centuries*.

the latter's dependence on the former. As Ian Levy points out, "there were no medieval commentators of any century who detached themselves from patristic authority and influence."[2] Many medieval interpreters engaged the early church fathers as if their predecessors were inspired, and so there are a lot of shared assumptions across these broad eras, even though there were plenty of differences of opinion. Key figures from these periods with important commentaries on Galatians include: Marius Victorinus, John Chrysostom, Jerome, Ambrosiaster, Augustine, and Thomas Aquinas, to name some of the most notable ones.

Patristic and medieval exegesis is often known for its interest in allegorical readings and other forms of reading that look beyond the literal for deeper spiritual meaning. With Paul's letters, however, this type of engagement occurred much less, presumably because Paul's meaning was conveyed through logic and argumentation, and because interpreters perceived that he was offering doctrinal truths more directly than narrative.[3]

Speaking of doctrine, commentaries from patristic and medieval interpreters were very sensitive to the way that Paul's statements about the Father, Jesus, and the Spirit, provide support for orthodox trinitarian theology and Chalcedonian Christology over and against various heretical teachings. In other words, Galatians, which is itself a polemical letter, is used in service of later debates within the history of Christianity. By no means is polemics strictly a hallmark of these periods, however. Every reading of Galatians is deployed against other interpretations. So, the issue is not whether battles are fought with the text, but which ones, and in those earliest Galatians commentaries we see interpreters fighting crucial doctrinal fights in real time.

2. Levy, *Letter to the Galatians*, 33.
3. Levy, *Letter to the Galatians*, 17.

As it pertains to the essence of what makes Galatians the unique letter that it is, though, the patristic and medieval interpreters found in it a sketch for the relationship of Israel's and the Church's Scriptures. On the one hand, there is continuity between them. God's purposes in salvation history were united by the promises that he made and the fulfillment that comes with the advent of Christ. Even though the reality of Christ was not fully disclosed in the OT, the saints of Israel put their faith in God's promises, which find their realization in Christ, and thus they stand in a continuity of faith with those who came to know Christ after his arrival.[4] On the other hand, these interpreters also recognized elements of discontinuity in history, such as the way that the time of the law gave way to an era of grace. However, this contrast was not so sharp. This is because "works of the law" for patristic and medieval interpreters usually did not refer to the entirety of the Mosaic law, but specifically to its *ceremonial* elements. Paul's statements about the law, then, are typically interpreted in these time periods as a call to eschew all of the rituals and customs of the Jewish people, including circumcision, because they have all been supplanted and replaced with the "superior" religion of Christianity. Yet the *moral* aspects of the Mosaic law continued to endure, and they were essential to the Christian living of those "made righteous" by faith—the father virtue that begets the other virtues. So then, in Galatians there is both continuity between the testaments in terms of faith, grace, and moral expectation, held together by promise and fulfillment, and also discontinuity with respect to Jewish ceremonial laws, customs, and rituals from the law.

---

4. Levy, *Letter to the Galatians*, 3, 31.

2. LUTHERAN/REFORMATIONAL READINGS

With the Reformation in the sixteenth century CE, there was a shift in reading Galatians as Paul's critique of human attempts to earn God's favor and to receive salvation through works. In this scheme, circumcision becomes one good work among many that won't lead to salvation. The key figure here, of course, is Martin Luther, whose interpretative approach to Galatians, and Paul more broadly, not only influenced Lutheranism, but also the broader Protestant movement.

Martin Luther was an Augustinian monk famously plagued by a guilty conscience. In particular, he was haunted by the idea that God was a just judge who would never accept him. That is, if the basis of that acceptance was his own ability to amass enough good works to please God. The stress on moral expectation in the medieval era had led to an emphasis on accumulating merit before God. As a result, a number of remedies were introduced by the Catholic church to address these types of concerns, such as indulgences, which provide a way for someone to essentially pay money to receive less punishment for their sins. This process was designed to ease the consciences of those who felt that their bad deeds were more numerous than their good ones, or that certain bad deeds were just too egregious that they would outweigh the good. In that religious context, Luther saw in Paul something refreshingly different. Specifically, it was the idea of justification by faith, rather than by works of the law, that fueled Luther to ignite the Reformation in protest to what medieval Catholicism had become. For Luther, justification by faith meant that there was nothing that could be done to earn God's righteousness. Instead, righteousness is not something one achieves, but is rather a status that God grants on the basis of faith, even as people remain imperfect sinners the rest of their earthly lives.

In Galatians, Luther found an emphasis on the gospel of Christ over and against the law. This came to be known as the "Law and Gospel contrast." The point of the law, for Luther, was to curtail sin and to convict people of their sin, so that they can come to embrace the good news—good cop, bad cop. The law was never meant to be observed perfectly, because sin prevents that from happening and because such striving would not impress God anyway. It is only by relying fully on the work of Christ that salvation comes, and the law serves to prompt such a need for a savior. Once people are justified by faith, the moral laws can become a guide for believers, but not as a back door to accruing favor with God. Thus, circumcision and law-observance are a few ways, among many, that people might think that they could merit righteousness before God, but in Luther's reading of Galatians, it is only by faith in Christ, trusting wholly in what he has done on our behalf, that one can be given the status of righteous.

3. NEW PERSPECTIVE READINGS

A new interpretative trend, called the New Perspective on Paul, emerged in the late twentieth century, which acknowledged that although Luther may have had good reasons to reject medieval Catholicism, the result is that he misunderstood ancient Judaism and thus misread Galatians in the process. Although there were important precursors to this perspective that paved the way for it,[5] the paradigm-shift really began with the 1977 publication of E. P. Sanders's *Paul and Palestinian Judaism*.

---

5. E.g., Davies, *Paul and Rabbinic Judaism*; Stendahl, *Paul among Jews and Gentiles*.

In his survey of primary sources from second temple Judaism, Sanders argued that we have misunderstood first-century Judaism because we have been reading Paul through Luther's battles. Ancient Jews were not medieval Catholics, and when the primary sources are closely engaged, Sanders argued, it becomes apparent that ancient Jews did not believe that they were earning their salvation through observing the law. Rather, the law was given to Israel after God graciously delivered them from Egypt at the exodus; grace, therefore, precedes the law.

Sanders argued further that second temple Jews had a distinctive "pattern of religion," which he termed "covenantal nomism." The role of the law, in this grid, was to govern the maintenance of covenantal life, but it did not relate to how someone got into the covenant or received God's grace, because the Jewish people were already in covenant with God and had thus already received his grace. In brief, the law governed "staying in" rather than "getting in." Far from being a "religion of works," then, Sanders argued that Judaism was a religion of grace.

So what was Paul's problem with Judaism exactly? Sanders wasn't entirely sure. As he articulates, Paul had to work backwards from his encounter with Christ. Paul came to recognize that Jesus was the solution, even if the plight had to be recognized retroactively from the kind of savior that Jesus was. In Sanders's famous words, which gets at the perplexing nature of things, the problem with Judaism for Paul is that it was not Christianity.[6]

Sanders's work became very influential, and it was his influence that led to the emergence of the so-called New Perspective on Paul, as championed by scholars like N. T. Wright and James D. G. Dunn.[7] What their work does, in

6. Sanders, *Paul and Palestinian Judaism*, 552.

7. Cf., e.g., Dunn, *New Perspective on Paul*; Wright, *Justification*.

their respective ways, is develop the insights from Sanders for a more developed reading of Paul. In particular, they argued that the "works of the law" in Galatians are ethnic boundary markers that separate Jews from gentiles (i.e., circumcision, Sabbath, food laws). Justification by faith is thus about how Jews and gentiles can come together under Christ despite their ethnic differences. So, in this reading of Galatians, Paul's concern is not with Judaism *per se*, or with earning salvation by works, but rather with critiquing a Jewish ethno-centrism that boxes out gentiles from full participation in the Christian communities as gentiles. Thus, Galatians is about how *gentiles* do not need to be circumcised, and so become Jews in the process, in order to be part of the early Jesus movement, because they are accepted as gentiles on the basis of faith just as Jews are.

4. APOCALYPTIC READINGS

The apocalyptic reading strategy aims to situate Paul within a particular strand of second temple Judaism known as apocalyptic Judaism, as gleaned from ancient Jewish apocalypses like 1 Enoch, 4 Ezra, 2 Baruch, and not to mention Daniel and Revelation, among others. The term "apocalyptic," despite what images it might conjure up today in terms of the cataclysmic end of the world, has to do with *unveiling* or *revealing* something previously hidden or undisclosed. As a result, those who espouse an apocalyptic reading of Paul, and indeed Galatians, stress the way that Paul views God doing something new in the Christ-event. The main proponent of this view was J. Louis Martyn, who fully articulated this reading in his magisterial commentary on Galatians.[8] Martyn's approach has also influenced the work

8. Martyn, *Galatians*.

of others, including Douglas Campbell, Martinus de Boer, Susan Eastman, and Beverly Gaventa.[9]

As a result of highlighting areas of newness in Galatians, the apocalyptic reading places much less emphasis on the continuity between the Old and New Testaments or indeed between Judaism and the early Christian movement. Instead, the main emphasis is on elements of discontinuity in the letter that highlight what is new after the arrival of Christ. This discontinuity is seen as framing the beginning and end of the letter, as the present evil age (Gal 1:4) gives way to an era of new creation (Gal 6:15). From within this perspective, it is noted that in Galatians 3, for example, Paul does not speak in the most glowing of terms regarding the giving of the law, and also seems to ignore the history of Israel altogether, imagining that the story goes straight from Abraham to Jesus with a slight detour involving Moses. Rather than the Christ-event arising as the climax of any "horizontal" developments within salvation history, it instead constituted a radical "vertical" inbreaking or invasion of God from outside.

In this way, the Christ-event was unprecedented, constituting a break with history and with all semblance of religion. In some ways we could refer to the apocalyptic reading as a radical Lutheran view because instead of a "Law and Gospel contrast" this reading espouses more of a "Religion and Gospel contrast." Paul's critique of gentile circumcision and "works of the law" for justification in Galatians, then, is not an attack on Judaism, but is part of his promotion of life in the new creation, which is outside of the religions of the old world to which believers have been crucified with Christ (Gal 6:14).

---

9. Campbell, *Deliverance of God*; de Boer, *Galatians*; Eastman, *Recovering Paul's Mother Tongue*; Gaventa, *Our Mother Saint Paul*.

5. COUNTER-IMPERIAL READINGS

Counter-Imperial readings understand the crisis surrounding circumcision in Galatia to have more to do with the political situation during the time of the Roman Empire. In particular, what prompted the appeal of circumcision was the way that it could provide gentile men with legal coverage from their local civic duties. The reason why circumcision would provide legal protection for gentile men is because everyone was expected to participate in the local cults, to honor the gods, and to honor Caesar. A gentile man leaving behind pagan beliefs and practices in favor of a budding Jewish movement centered on Jesus had no legal recourse for doing so. Their lack of participation in local cults is seen as treasonous and seditious. And yet, Jews were free to practice their own religion (cf. Josephus, *Ant.* 16:162–165), and in some sense they were exempt from participating in the imperial cult, though they did participate in it in distinct ways, such as through the temple tax.[10] It is this dynamic of gentiles finding themselves socially dislocated—no longer wishing to be pagan but not being "Jewish enough" to claim exemption—that prompts the Galatian crisis, according to this view.

Perhaps the initial proponent of this reading, broadly conceived, was Bruce Winter, which was later developed by Justin Hardin and Brigette Kahl in their own unique ways.[11] For Hardin, the gentiles in Galatia were continuing to participate in the imperial cult, as they formerly did, after their embrace of Christ, in order to alleviate the social tension of being uncircumcised. Paul's shadowy opponents, according to this view, wanted the Galatians to join fully in with

---

10. Hardin, *Galatians*, 109.

11. Winter, "Imperial Cult"; Hardin, *Galatians*; Kahl, *Galatians Re-Imagined*.

the local Jewish communities, but that could only happen if they underwent circumcision.[12] Paul's argument, then, is read as prohibiting the Galatians from pursuing either alternative: receiving circumcision or continuing to participate in the imperial cult.[13] Counter-Imperial readings commonly see Paul directly engaging imperial practices and ideology, even in places where scholars typically think the Mosaic law is in view (cf. Gal 4:10), or they see Paul doing so more subtly, such as how Kahl views the Mosaic law as being co-opted by imperial ideology in her reading of the letter, which emphasizes the Galatians as conquered peoples of the Roman Empire.

6. PAUL WITHIN JUDAISM READINGS

The final reading to include in this brief survey is what is known as the "Paul within Judaism" perspective, as advocated by scholars like Paula Fredriksen, Lloyd Gaston, Caroline Johnson Hodge, Mark Nanos, Matthew Thiessen, and others.[14] This reading strategy builds upon the New Perspective on Paul in some ways, particularly the insistence that Pauline scholarship has not fully appreciated Paul's Jewish context, and it is often labeled "the Radical New Perspective." Proponents of this view are particularly keen to uphold a distinctive sense of Jewish identity for Paul, especially in the light of the post-Holocaust environment in which we read Paul today. Scholars in this school of thought tend to stress that Paul has been so absorbed into the theology and tradition of Christianity that we need to learn to "let Paul be weird" and view him as "[j]ust one Jew

12. Hardin, *Galatians*, 112.

13. Hardin, *Galatians*, 141.

14. Fredriksen, *Paul*; Gaston, *Paul and the Torah*; Hodge, *If Sons*; Nanos, *Irony of Galatians*; Thiessen, *Jewish Paul*.

living his life and following his perceived calling amid the diversity and richness of first-century Judaism."[15]

The main tenet of this reading is perhaps that Judaism is never a foil for Paul, whether in terms of having outdated customs, legalism, ethnocentrism, being a "religion," or anything else. There was nothing wrong with Judaism, because, in fact, Paul was a Jew, and remained thoroughly Jewish after his encounter with Christ. This perspective thus stresses that Paul was a law-observant Jew, and expected that all other Jews in the early Jesus movement would be too. Paul's seemingly critical comments about the law, then, do not apply to how Jews relate to the law, but apply rather to the way that gentiles relate to it.[16] The main reason for this is because Paul's audiences were gentile, and thus the topic of Jewish law observance and a Jewish relationship to the law is not in focus.

With the issue of circumcision in Galatians, then, the concern is specifically with gentiles and not with the ongoing Jewish practice of it. Some proponents within the Paul within Judaism school contend that adult circumcision as a means of conversion was not a valid category.[17] For Thiessen, in particular, the only kind of circumcision that Paul believed was valid was the circumcision of male infants on the eighth-day after their birth (Gen 17:12; cf. Phil 3:5; Jub. 15:25–26), and so the problem with circumcision in Galatians is that it was not effective for adults.[18]

Additionally, this reading strategy hangs a lot on Paul's pneumatology because the Spirit is the specific solution to the problem of being a gentile. The Jews were in covenant

15. Thiessen, *Jewish Paul*, 35; cf. Novenson, "Our Apostles, Ourselves."

16. Fredriksen, *Paul*, 122.

17. Cf. Fredriksen, *Paul*, 128–29, 158.

18. Thiessen, *Jewish Paul*, 98.

with God, they had the benefits of eighth-day circumcision, as well as the gift of the Torah and the sacrificial system in the temple, etc., but what was there for gentiles? The Paul within Judaism school typically stresses that the Spirit, or *pneuma*, changes the DNA of gentile Christ-followers and makes them children of Abraham, and thus as people who have the Spirit, they are empowered to follow the Messiah outside of their possession of the law.[19] Because the Spirit is often believed to resolve the gentile problem, some within this broader reading of Paul argue that Paul held to a different way of salvation for Jews (often known as a *Sonderweg*).[20] Differing paths to salvation is not a consistent feature of every Paul within Judaism reading, however, and some acknowledge that Paul thinks that both Jews and gentiles were in need of Jesus.[21]

ASSESSING THE READING STRATEGIES

In this brief overview, I've not been exhaustive by any means with respect to each of these views, or indeed with respect to all of the ways that Galatians has been read. Obviously much more could be said, but this is enough for us to dig in to the letter. Before concluding this overview of reading strategies, however, I'll now offer some quick comments on each strategy in terms of what I see as commonalities and differences with own my approach to reading Galatians.

With patristic and medieval readings of Galatians, I affirm that Paul articulates elements of continuity and discontinuity with respect to the time before and after the advent of Christ. Moreover, I think there's good reason to

19. Hodge, *If Sons*; Thiessen, *Jewish Paul*, 101–12.

20. Gaston, *Paul and the Torah*. Cf. Boccaccini, *Paul's Three Paths to Salvation*.

21. Cf. Thiessen, *Jewish Paul*, 150–51, 155.

see how Paul's Christology lends itself to the development of orthodoxy, although it would be anachronistic to represent Paul as espousing, let's say, the specific tenets of the Nicene Creed, of course. But against patristic and medieval readings, the elements of discontinuity that they discerned in Galatians were often overemphasized in the wrong direction. With respect to the discontinuity associated with the law in Galatians, that should not be taken as a wholesale critique of Judaism as a religion replaced with Christianity (i.e., "supersessionism"). Part of the problem that often led to such a conclusion was that these interpreters, likely due to their own polemical contexts with Jewish people, viewed Paul as combating "Jewish opponents of the Christian faith,"[22] ignoring how Paul's opponents were themselves part of the nascent Christian movement (cf. Gal 6:12).

When it comes to Lutheran readings, I agree that Paul does not believe that anyone can earn God's favor. Being righteous is a status, a legal verdict from within a law-court, designating someone as "in the right" or "innocent." That is fundamentally what I think justification means for Paul, and that way of conceiving it owes a lot to the broader Lutheran approach to Paul. Contrary to Lutheran readings of Galatians, however, I don't think that Paul is addressing the topic of whether humans can earn God's favor through "good works." To be sure, the Pauline letters do address the broader topic of "works" elsewhere (cf., e.g., Eph 2:8–10), but Galatians, in my view, does not have its sights set on such a wide target. Instead, it seems to me that the issues in Galatians concern the entirety of the law, and specifically the law as a Jewish way of life. Thus, I don't think that "the Law and Gospel contrast" is the best way to characterize what Paul says about the law in Galatians.

22. Levy, *Letter to the Galatians*, 5.

As for Sanders and the New Perspective on Paul, I agree that second temple Judaism was not hopelessly legalistic or devoid of grace, although much more needs to be said to nuance what it means to say that ancient Jews believed in grace, since that was by no means configured the exact same way by all.[23] I agree that when Paul speaks about "works of the law," he does not refer to "good works" generally, but rather specifically to what the law of Moses prescribes and requires. It seems to me that matters of friction with gentile communities are likely top of mind in Galatians (i.e., circumcision, Sabbath-keeping, and dietary laws), but not exclusively so, and I do not think that Paul was critiquing his fellow Jews for being too ethnocentric. Thus, the "works of the law," in my view, refer to the whole Mosaic law as it governs Jewish covenantal life, and the pressing question in Galatians seems to me to be how they do or don't relate to gentiles who were joining a Jewish movement centered on Israel's Messiah.

Turning to the apocalyptic readings, I agree with its proponents that the Christ-event was unique and that it necessarily changed aspects about how Paul understood God, the law, and the world. Galatians certainly contains elements of discontinuity that align themselves with the new thing that God is doing in Christ. Against this apocalyptic perspective, however, discontinuity and newness in Galatians is often overemphasized. As a result of their appropriate desire to uphold the Christ-event as a unique revelatory act of God, apocalyptic interpreters have too sharply disconnected the Christ-event from the way Paul understands God's purposes in Israel's history. As we will see in chapters 6–7 in particular, I think that apocalyptic readers are right to highlight that in Galatians 3 Paul's argument is rooted in a set of claims about the law having a

23. See esp. Barclay, *Paul & the Gift*.

temporary role. But they too often make it seem as if Paul does not want to affirm, in Galatians at least, that the law was God-given. And moreover, they tend to stress that Paul shows a lack of interest in Israel's complex history when he addresses the purpose of the law, especially since the "seed" promised to Abraham isn't the people of Israel, but Christ himself (Gal 3:16). I admit that Paul, for rhetorical purposes, rushes over Israel's history and only offers a few bullet points, but I would contend that Paul has the shape of Israel's history in mind as he makes his arguments from Gal 3:6—4:7. Specifically, as I will argue in chapter 6, it seems that Paul overviews Israel's history three times (i.e., Gal 3:6-14, 3:15-29, and 4:1-7) with each mini-history addressing the role of the law in relation to the fulfillment of promises made to Abraham. It's noteworthy to me, in this regard, that the second-century heretic, Marcion, someone who heavily edited Paul's letters to remove references to the God of the OT and Israel's history, eliminated Gal 3:6-9; 3:14a; and 3:15-25.[24] This suggests that even though Paul rushes over Israel's history, it was still too much for Marcion. So I contend that Israel's history is reflected there, and even more so than Marcion may have recognized.

Thus, the discontinuity in Galatians should not be stressed as much as apocalyptic interpreters do, because for Paul it is the same covenant God of the OT who is the one doing the unexpected thing, just like he always said he would.[25] That God would act in surprising ways is a "known unknown." Indeed, this is in keeping with how apocalyptic Jews seem to have understood history,[26] and thus the term "apocalyptic" for this contemporary approach to Galatians

24. Levy, *Letter to the Galatians*, 19.

25. Paraphrasing N. T. Wright from personal conversation.

26. The disjunctive elements in Galatians cannot all be derived from apocalypticism; see L. Williams, "Disjunction in Paul."

is a bit of a misnomer. The way that the notion of "apocalyptic" is often articulated by these interpreters has much more to do with the theology of the twentieth-century Swiss theologian Karl Barth, which is not inappropriate in itself, if only they claimed to be offering a *Barthian reading* of Paul. I have also criticized this reading strategy in the past for not being sufficiently apocalyptic in terms of recognizing themes common to both apocalyptic literature and Galatians, namely those that arise from common social settings of suffering and crisis, which so often fuel apocalyptic imagination and hope.[27] As we will see, that is an apocalyptic element that I think is really important for reading Galatians.

As it pertains to the Counter-Imperial readings of Galatians, it seems right to me that circumcision *per se* is not the concern. Instead, the letter is best read in the light of the social and political reasons that circumcision would become an option worth pursuing for adult gentile men. This seems to fit the dynamics of social tension and external pressure that Paul alludes to and explicitly addresses at a few different instances in the letter, but it also helps to explain why grown men would be keen to undergo such a procedure. Yet I do not go as far as most Counter-Imperial readings do down this road. In particular, I'm less inclined to find the influence of Roman imperial ideology on the crisis in Galatia beyond the potential issue of social pressure, as we will see in chapter 4. I don't think that Paul alludes to pagan practices (cf. Gal 4:10) in such a way as to suggest that the gentiles in Galatia were continuing to participate in the imperial cult as they geared up to receive circumcision,

---

27. Dunne, "Suffering and Covenantal Hope." More recently, Scott (*Apocalyptic Letter*) has compared Galatians to the Epistle of Enoch, and he contends that Galatians shares much of the same form and features with that apocalyptic text.

or that Paul had some type of coded message against the power structures of the Empire.

With respect to the final reading strategy, Paul within Judaism, I affirm that the central issues in Galatians are gentile issues, and that Paul not only thinks that the gentile men do not need to receive circumcision, but moreover that they should not receive it. I also agree that Paul remained a Jew, and did not attempt to abrogate Jewish law observance. However, I do have a few areas of disagreement with this perspective. To start, it does not seem to me that Paul thought that the circumcision of adults was ineffective, or that proselyte conversion was impossible. If it were the case that Paul's gripe with adult circumcision was that it wasn't eighth-day circumcision, then all he would need to do is say that explicitly and the debate would be over. Because Paul's argument in Galatians is actually fairly complex, if not actually circuitous, it would seem that he did not think that the timing of circumcision would settle the matter. In fact, Paul doesn't argue as if circumcision is ineffective.[28] Instead, he argues that circumcision obligates a person to "the whole law" and "cuts them off" from Christ (Gal 5:2–4).

A more fundamental disagreement with the Paul within Judaism perspective, though, is that I don't believe that what Paul has to say about the law's role in history in Galatians is focused exclusively on how the law relates to gentiles. In fact, I think the exact opposite point is true, because the law was given to Israel, and *why it was given to them* seems to be one of the questions that Paul is trying to answer. The implications of what Paul says about the law thus apply to Jews, not least because Paul was a Jew, but also because arguably his most controversial statements about the law in Galatians involve his own relationship to the law, and he says them to Peter, a fellow Jew, addressing things

28. Rightly, Dibley, "The Making and Unmaking of Jews."

they each know to be true as Jewish followers of Jesus (cf. Gal 2:15–21).

Now, I fully respect that we need to "let Paul be weird" when doing proper history, and avoid trying to make him into a "law-free Christian." That is totally true, but this point seems to me to be one-sided. A simplification of the logic seems to go like this: Paul ought to be weird in relation to contemporary Christianity, but he must not be too weird with respect to first-century Judaism. This strikes me as a refashioned form of the "criterion of dissimilarity" from historical Jesus studies, where certain scholars used to contend that something in the Gospels is more likely to be historical and attributed to Jesus, rather than later tradition, if what he says is unique with respect to the Judaism of his time and the Christian tradition that developed in his name. The problem with this criterion for historicity, of course, is that Jesus could neither be *influenced* nor an *influence*, which makes no sense. In the Paul within Judaism version of dissimilarity, it seems that if a reading of Paul aligns too much with later Christian thinking, especially with respect to what Paul says about the law, it must not be historical. Even as the Paul within Judaism interpreters grant how diverse second temple Judaism was, there still seems to be a limited range of what qualifies as "within Judaism" in this field.[29] Thus, in my view, in the appeal to "let Paul be weird," there seems to be a pre-determination of just how weird Paul can be. I think we have to be open to the historical possibility that Paul's approach to the law changed, to some degree, in the light of the advents of the Messiah and the Spirit. To claim otherwise is to insist on an essentialist view of what Judaism is. Why couldn't Paul hold to a distinctive, even weird, view of the law as a Jew?

29. Cf. Scott, *Apocalyptic Letter*.

As a concluding thought, then, I don't see myself aligning neatly with any of the reading strategies when I approach Galatians. Instead, I draw eclectically from the insights of each one, insofar as I might find some of their observations, arguments, and correctives compelling. As well, I don't regard any of these readings as being completely off-base either. They all provide important reminders that Galatians is elusive and resists being neatly placed in a box, no matter how nice the packaging. You, dear reader, may situate yourself comfortably within any one of these approaches (or others), and that is entirely fine by me, but don't feel like you need to pick a camp either. I don't intend to be overly polemical or apologetic, but hopefully I can offer some modest insights to stimulate further your own reading of, and reflection on, this remarkable letter.

REFLECTIONS

1. Which reading strategy or strategies seem to make the most sense to you presently?
2. Do any of the reading strategies represent how you have thought about Galatians in the past?

3

PAUL'S INITIAL VISIT TO GALATIA

As we dig into the nature of the Galatian crisis, the rest of the present book will unfold in a somewhat chronological fashion, beginning with what we can know about Paul's ministry among the Galatians. Based on scattered evidence from the letter itself, we can attempt to reconstruct aspects of their first encounter, which will be supplemented with other sources of evidence, like the book of Acts. The impression that all of the evidence provides is that, although Paul's ministry to Galatia was filled with turmoil, it was a fruitful time for the expansion of the gospel.

THE GALATIANS EMBRACED PAUL IN HIS WEAKNESS

In two instances in Galatians Paul appeals to his initial interactions with his readers, where he wishes that things were like they used to be. In both Gal 3:1–5 and Gal 4:12–20 we get glimpses of that first meeting before Paul shifts his attention to the present crisis. Let's start with the latter of the two passages to see how Paul does this.

> **Gal 4:12–15:** Be like me, because even I was like you, siblings, I beg of you. You did me no wrong. You know that it was because of a weakness of the flesh that I proclaimed the gospel to you formerly, and your temptation in my flesh you did not despise or spit out, but you received me as an angel from God, even Christ Jesus. Where then is your blessing? For I testify to you that, if possible, you would have gouged out your eyes and given them to me.

I stop here at verse 15 because we already start to see a break in their relationship when Paul asks, "Where then is your blessing?" The focus on the present crisis is then characteristic of the rest of this section in verses 16–20, which is the subject of the next chapter.

Although Paul starts Gal 4:12–20 with a direct call for the Galatians to be like him, he does not explicitly state what he wants them to imitate. Given the nature of the crisis of circumcision and law observance, many have taken this to mean that Paul wants the Galatians to be law-free like he has become since encountering Christ. This interpretation would not sit well with the Paul within Judaism crowd, since in their view Paul remains law observant as a Jewish follower of Jesus. But one need not subscribe to the broader Paul within Judaism perspective to find an appeal to being law-free off topic for what follows. As Paul goes on to narrate in verses 13–15, the Galatians originally embraced Paul and had a bond with him during a time of "weakness," and so Paul may be asking them to imitate him with respect to his endurance of hardships. Paul appears to be reminding the Galatians of those initial experiences as a personal appeal for loyalty, and hence the call for imitation, which also makes sense if the newly developed crisis contains its own form of hardships (as we will see in chapter 4).

As Paul recounts, his travel plans in Galatia were originally interrupted. The reason he proclaimed the gospel to them was "because of a weakness of the flesh" (Gal 4:13). What was this "weakness"? We are not told specifically, but many wonder whether it may have been a type of illness, perhaps a chronic condition or disability which led to an increase in symptoms as he was traveling. It has been proposed that maybe Paul had malaria, poor eye sight (*ophthalmia*), or epilepsy. As people try to identify the specific malady that Paul experienced, some have also wondered if Paul's "thorn in the flesh" from 2 Cor 12:1–10 was a related condition.

Whatever the "weakness" was, Paul says that it was a "temptation" for the Galatians. What about Paul's condition would they have found tempting? Most likely it was the temptation to reject Paul and not allow him to enter their homes. As he says, they did not reject him, but instead they received him as an angel, and even as Christ himself. But it is not simply that they did not reject him, they also did not *spit him out*, the Greek says. Our English translations typically do not render the verb *ekptuō* this way. They opt instead for a synonym of rejection, as we see typified in the NRSVue: "you did not scorn or despise me" (Gal 4:14). But the Greek word *ekptuō* is what we call an onomatopoeia, meaning that the word sounds like the action itself. Try to pronounce that word to yourself, and you'll see what I mean, just please avoid spitting into the book (especially if this isn't your own copy). I think it's important to retain "spitting" in my translation because spitting was an obvious way to communicate rejection, but also culturally it was an *apotropaic* practice, meaning that it was designed to keep people away with particular diseases like epilepsy and/or anyone oppressed by demons. If someone shows up to a community beaten and battered, for example, you wouldn't be quick to welcome them because you don't know what group of people that person has ticked off, let alone what demons or deities they may have angered to end up like that. But Paul is saying that the Galatians did not give in to this temptation to reject him or to spit him out, but instead they embraced him. Rather than treating him like he had a demon, the Galatians welcomed him as an angel, even Christ Jesus.

Whereas the reference to spitting could support the epileptic interpretation of the "weakness of the flesh," I think that the way they embraced Paul like Jesus suggests an alternative interpretation. There are at least two reasons that I think that the "weakness of the flesh" was not an illness, but rather the result of ill-treatment.[1] First, in Galatians Paul refers to his own experience of persecution explicitly (Gal 5:11) in a letter in which "persecution" is repeated multiple times: Paul himself persecuted early Jesus followers (Gal 1:13, 23), the children of the flesh persecute the children of the Spirit (Gal 4:29), and Paul's opponents promote circumcision in order to avoid persecution (Gal 6:12). Second, Paul links his suffering with the suffering of Jesus: he is persecuted for the cross (Gal 5:11), and he bears in his body the "marks of Jesus" (Gal 6:17), which are likely the physical marks of his ill-treatment for the cause of Christ. So, when Paul says that the Galatians received him like Christ in his weakness, that connection seems to suggest that Paul had experienced hostile opposition to the gospel, which weakened him.

Before shifting over completely to address the present crisis in the rest of Gal 4:12–20, Paul reminds them once more of what a "blessing" it was to be in a state of mutuality

1. Goddard and Cummins, "Ill or Ill-Treated?"

and reciprocity when they were together (Gal 4:15). Paul says that they would have gouged out their own eyes and given them to him. The Galatians clearly would have gone to great lengths for Paul, but things have changed. Most likely Paul does not use this example because he had poor eyesight (*ophthalmia*), as some have suggested, but instead this may have been a way to express generosity, as if Paul had said, "you would have given me the shirt off your back." As Paul mentions in verse 17, the Galatians were originally zealous for what Paul brought to them when he was with them. Because that zeal has gone away, Paul feels like his efforts in Galatia may have failed. He describes this like having birth pains that won't actually lead to a healthy baby (Gal 4:19). Although in Paul's convoluted metaphor, his own birth pains are not for the growth of the Galatians in his own womb, but rather for the growth of the Messiah in the womb(s) of the Galatians. Setting aside the difficulty of conceptualizing this mixed metaphor, the language of gestation being compromised at the time of birth conveys through maternal imagery Paul's relationship to the Galatians as the founding missionary who brought the message of the Messiah to them.[2] Just as spitting and tearing out eyes in this context does not prove that Paul's "weakness of the flesh" was epilepsy or poor eye sight, neither do his birth pains suggest, I say with tongue in cheek, that his initial "weakness of the flesh" was morning sickness! In all seriousness, though, these references to sharing eyes, having zeal, and portraying Paul as a mother, further highlight the strong bond that they initially had with each other.

---

2. For more on this dynamic, see Kok and Dunne, "Participation in Christ and Missional Dynamics."

Paul's Initial Visit to Galatia

THE GALATIANS EMBRACED PAUL'S PORTRAYAL OF THE CRUCIFIED MESSIAH

Turning to Gal 3:1–5, we find the other extended passage where Paul reminds the Galatians of when he first visited them.

> **Gal 3:1–3:** O foolish Galatians, who bewitched you—before whose eyes Jesus Christ was publicly portrayed as crucified? This alone do I want to learn from you: did you receive the Spirit by works of the law or by hearing with faith? Are you foolish like this: beginning by the Spirit are you now perfected by the flesh?

I stop with verse 3 because the question: "are you now perfected by the flesh?" begins to shift away from the initial encounter with Paul into the present crisis in Galatia. When Paul starts by calling the Galatians "foolish" and "bewitched," he speaks to the discrepancy between that initial visit and the present situation. In particular, Paul reminds them of how they first received the Spirit of God by "hearing with faith," which implies a setting of proclamation.

During that proclamation, Paul says, their eyes also beheld the public portrayal of Jesus Christ crucified (Gal 3:1). But how could this be true? The Galatians lived in central Anatolia (more on this later), and so they were not literally present at Golgotha when Jesus was crucified. Various proposals have been made to explain what else this could mean. Some have said maybe Paul means that the Scriptures so clearly anticipate the sufferings of Christ that they could "see" him crucified as they read them (or had the Scriptures read/recited to them by Paul). Others have suggested that maybe Paul drew images of Jesus as crucified to supplement his teaching, or perhaps Paul acted out the crucifixion in a theatrical performance. The most common suggestion, though, is that Paul's preaching about Jesus was so vivid and compelling that it was as if they were witnessing the very things he taught about.

Yet there is another view that I think does better justice to this seemingly random comment. To be sure, Paul undeniably taught about Jesus's crucifixion when he was in Galatia, but I think he has something more in view regarding his time with them. Recall how we have already seen that Paul's travels to Galatia were disrupted by a "weakness of the flesh" in which the Galatians welcomed him as if he were Christ Jesus (Gal 4:13–14), and that Paul makes a strong connection between his suffering and Christ's suffering elsewhere in Galatians (Gal 5:11; 6:17). In addition to these two things, Paul also strongly identifies with the cross in such a way that he claims to have been crucified with Christ (Gal 2:19–20; cf. 5:24) and crucified to the world (Gal 6:14). When Paul says that the Galatians saw Jesus portrayed as crucified during his original proclamation, I think we should recognize that even here he is referring to the way that *his own suffering* revealed Christ crucified to them.[3] What makes this argument even more compelling is that it's just two verses earlier where Paul says that he is crucified with Christ and that Christ now lives in him (Gal 2:19–20). Thus, both passages, where Paul reflects on his initial ministry among the Galatians (Gal 3:1–5; 4:12–20), acknowledge in their respective ways that Paul's ministry in Galatia was occasioned by Christlike suffering.

EXPLICIT REFERENCES TO PAUL'S ORIGINAL PROCLAMATION

What else can we glean from Galatians about Paul's original proclamation in Galatia? Given the parallels between Gal

3. Davis, "Meaning of ΠΡΟΕΓΡΑΦΗ."

3:1–5 and 4:12–20, we have to imagine that Paul instructed the Galatians on the topic of suffering itself. This would have been a necessary component of Paul's gospel, not least in order to make sense of a crucified Messiah and his suffering apostle. We may assume that he taught them, then, about how to make sense of their own suffering and hardship for the sake of the gospel as well.

In addition to those sections of Galatians that give us a glimpse into Paul's initial visit, Paul also makes further offhand comments about the nature of his proclamation when he was with them—the sorts of things that the Galatians "heard with faith" when they first received the Spirit. Paul does not mention enough for us to reconstruct his message completely, but we are given some insights into what he likely shared with them. These passages are Gal 1:8–9; 1:13–14; and 5:19–21. Starting with the first of these, Paul writes:

> **Gal 1:8-9:** But even if we or an angel from heaven might preach a gospel to you that is contrary to what we proclaimed to you, let him be accursed. As we have told you, and now I say again, if someone might preach a gospel to you that is contrary to what you received, let him be accursed.

This passage implies all sorts of teaching about Israel's Messiah, although Paul does not reiterate the specifics. But Paul does affirm here that he indicated to them that deviation from that teaching would not be tolerated.

Carrying on with the next one:

> **Gal 1:13-14:** For you heard about my former life in Judaism, that I was persecuting the church of God to the uttermost and was trying to destroy it, and I was advancing in Judaism beyond many contemporaries in my generation, being

> exceedingly zealous for the traditions of my ancestors.

With this passage, Paul speaks of formerly participating in "Judaism." You might be tempted to think that this passage completely undermines the "Paul within Judaism" perspective, but you'd be wrong. The translation "Judaism" is really misleading because Paul is not referring to a religion that he departed from in favor of another, or indeed in favor of no religion at all, as apocalyptic Paul proponents might say. Although there aren't many good options for a different translation, we should recognize that Paul doesn't mean that he stopped being a Jew, but rather that he stopped being a certain kind of Jew. The kind of Jew that he stopped being at the time of his call was the kind that was so committed to opposing Hellenization or any perceived drift away from Jewish customs among Jewish people.[4] This commitment is what led him to violence, but he no longer held on to that perspective after his encounter with the Messiah.

For our purposes in this chapter, it is not clear how much of what follows about Paul's transformation that the Galatians would have heard before (nor whether they heard this originally from Paul or from his opponents). We can't really know for sure, but I don't see why this information wouldn't have been part of what Paul originally shared with them. Perhaps he is reminding them of his transformation, which he told them about when he was with them. But the new disclosure (cf. Gal 1:11 "I make known to you") is how his transformation relates to his relationship with Jerusalem and the authorities there, since that is the focus of the autobiography (which I will say more about in chapters 4–5).

Finally, in Gal 5:19–21, Paul writes:

---

4. Novenson, "Paul's Former Occupation in *Ioudaismos*."

> **Gal 5:19–21:** Now the works of the flesh are revealed, which are sexual immorality, impurity, sensuality, idolatry, sorcery, hostilities, strife, zeal, anger, rivalries, divisions, factions, envy, drunkenness, orgies, and things like these, which I tell you in advance, even as I told you before, that those doing such things will not inherit the kingdom of God.

The list of some representative works of the flesh is an important part of Paul's argument, and is the immediate foil for the fruit of the Spirit that follows. It is worth noting that Paul acknowledges that, when he was in Galatia, he addressed the topic of how fleshly vices will keep people from inheriting the kingdom of God: "even as I told you before." Undoubtedly, Paul addressed plenty of other things while he was in Galatia, but these are some of the things that he chooses to remind the Galatians about in his letter.

RELEVANCE THEORY

A helpful way to think about why Paul doesn't address his visit and original message more clearly and fully is due to something called relevance theory.[5] This theory reminds us that whenever there is shared knowledge and shared experiences, a lot goes unstated and is assumed. So, when we are reading Galatians, it is not simply the case that we are listening to one side of a phone conversation, as it were, trying to imagine what the other person is saying. Relevance theory reminds us that even if we did know what the other side was saying, we'd still have a disadvantage because we won't know all of the insider information—the things that remain assumed without ever needing to be stated.

---

5. For more on this, see Brown, *Scripture as Communication*, 24–27.

One of my favorite illustrations of how relevance theory works comes from the film, *Independence Day*, starring Will Smith, which was a summer blockbuster from 1996. For our purposes, I want to draw your attention to the presidential speech delivered by US President Thomas Whitmore (Bill Pullman) to a group of soldiers at an Air Force base during a crucial point in the film.

> Good morning . . . Good morning. In less than an hour aircraft from here will join others from around the world. And you will be launching the largest aerial battle in the history of mankind—mankind, that word should have new meaning for all of us today. We can't be consumed by our petty differences anymore. We will be united in our common interest. Perhaps it's fate that today is the Fourth of July, and you will once again be fighting for our freedom, not from tyranny, oppression, or persecution, but from annihilation. We're fighting for our right to live, to exist. And should we win the day, the Fourth of July will no longer be known as an American holiday, but as the day when the world declared in one voice, "We will not go quietly into the night; we will not vanish without a fight! We're going to live on; we're going to survive. Today we celebrate our Independence Day!"

I have intentionally avoided telling you anything about this film beyond its name, a couple of the actors in it, and the fact that a speech is given by a fictional US President at an air force base. If you know the film, you know exactly what this speech *is about*, but if this is your first exposure to it, you might assume that the speech is simply about international unity in the face of impending war. That's correct as far as it goes, but notice how the opposition is never *explicitly* stated. Who will these soldiers be fighting against? Every character in the film knows, and every viewer who has seen the film knows too, but the speech never says. Despite that fact, the speech is actually all about one thing—aliens! Aliens have invaded the planet and are blowing up cities all over the world. Why doesn't President Whitmore say anything about aliens then? The answer is relevance theory.

With respect to Galatians, then, Paul gives us glimpses into his initial visit, sometimes referencing the interactions overtly and talking about his message, but there is a lot more that he could have shared and yet doesn't because of relevance theory. Acknowledging this is not a way for us to get away with making arguments from silence about what Paul could have said and did. Rather we should consider relevance theory as a way to deploy our chastened imaginations to fill in some of the gaps in our knowledge.

There must also be some things that Paul does mention in Galatians, which reflect his initial experiences with them, but which he fails to overtly connect to his initial visit. One such example comes in Gal 2:10, where Paul says that the Jerusalem apostles asked Paul to "remember the poor" in his ministry to gentiles, and he acknowledges that he was already doing this. It would be strange for Paul to include this fact if it was not the case that Paul taught the Galatians about the importance of remembering the poor, or if he did not himself do something for the poor while he was there. Otherwise, he'd be telling on himself. Corroboration of this point comes from outside of Galatians, where we find an overt reference to a potentially-related matter that Paul taught the Galatians. At the end of 1 Corinthians, Paul has this to say about the collection for the saints.

> **1 Cor 16:1–4:** Now concerning the collection for the saints: just as I ordered the churches of Galatia, so also you should do. On the first day of the week, let each of you, as he might prosper,

> set something aside and store it, so that whenever I come, there will not be any collecting. Whenever I arrive, I will send, along with these letters, whomever you approve to carry your gift to Jerusalem. If it might be worthwhile that I go also, they will go with me.

Paul states here that he taught "the churches of Galatia" (just as he refers to them in Gal 1:2) about a plan to take up a monetary collection. This collection was intended for the saints in Jerusalem, which would seemingly function to show that Paul's ministry to the gentiles was not disconnected from Jerusalem. One way that Paul may have chosen to "remember the poor" as he was charged in Gal 2:10 is through implementing this collection plan. This would not mean that "remembering the poor" was merely shorthand for this collection, however. This comment in 1 Corinthians about instructing the Galatians on the collection, and how to go about it, suggests that this was another element of Paul's initial ministry in Galatia, since he does not discuss the collection in the letter. If Paul taught them about the collection, he very likely taught them about the importance of caring for the poor (Gal 2:10), whether or not the collection itself was designed to address that very issue.

Another example of something mentioned in Galatians that is not directly connected to Paul's initial ministry, but should be taken to reflect it, comes at the end of Galatians 3. We may assume, I would argue, on the basis of the central baptismal text, that Paul and his entourage baptized the Galatians.[6]

> **Gal 3:26–29:** For you are sons of God through faith in Christ Jesus. For as many as those among

---

6. To avoid any confusion, I am not suggesting that Gal 3:26–29 is part of a baptismal liturgy that Paul recited during baptisms, as many scholars have asserted without clear basis.

> you are baptized into Christ, you put on Christ.
> There is no Jew nor Greek, there is no slave nor
> free, there is no male and female; for you all are
> one in Christ Jesus. And if you belong to Christ,
> then you are the seed of Abraham, heirs according to the promise.

Paul is undoubtedly theologizing in this baptismal text as part of his response to the crisis (and so we will need to address this again in chapter 6), but here we just need to observe that Paul's appeal to the experience of baptism assumes that the Galatians were baptized, and who else would have baptized them? Paul doesn't say this explicitly, but most likely the initial converts at least were baptized while Paul was there, and presumably subsequently others continued to be baptized after he left. Because there is a hierarchical authority conveyed in baptism—one person with authority to do so baptizes someone else—it is likely that when Paul refers to their baptism it was a way of reminding them of, and reinforcing, Paul's apostolic authority over them (which seems to be questioned).[7] Allegiance to the authority of the one performing baptism is signaled in 1 Cor 1:10–17, when certain members in Corinth held allegiances to the apostle who baptized them, or when John the Baptist suggests that actually Jesus should baptize *him* and not the other way around (Matt 3:14).[8] So, the reference to the Galatians' own baptism would not only remind them of Paul's initial visit, but also his authority as expressed in the ritual act itself. Furthermore, the language of sonship and the references to social categories like Jew/Greek, slave/free, and "male and female" in Gal 3:26–29, highlight that baptism is a kinship-making rite. The hierarchical relationship between the baptizer and the one baptized, then, is like

7. Yuh, "Analysing Paul's Reference to Baptism."
8. Yuh, "Analysing Paul's Reference to Baptism," 489.

that of a parent and child.[9] This implication of baptism fills out the meaning of Paul's maternal imagery in Gal 4:19 and the notion that the Galatians are children of Paul, which is a connection that can be made with the help of relevance theory.

WHERE IN GALATIA DID PAUL MINISTER?

As we have seen, there are some fascinating insights into Paul's initial ministry in Galatia within the letter itself, but where exactly in Galatia did Paul conduct this ministry? We know that Paul wrote to "the churches of Galatia" (Gal 1:2), and that he refers to his audience as "Galatians" (Gal 3:1). But where exactly was Galatia? For this we need to bring in the evidence from the book of Acts.

There's actually a fairly well-worn debate in scholarship about the location of these churches because the Roman province of Galatia was a fairly large region within ancient Anatolia (modern-day Turkey/Türkiye). The way the debate typically goes is that either Paul wrote to the northern part of the province in the mid-50s CE, or he wrote to the southern part in the late 40s CE. Scholarship has tended to divide into two camps (northern and late, or southern and early), but there is also the possibility of a southern destination and a later date. The southern destination *allows* for the earlier date, but does not require it.

What turns this into a debate is not strictly what Paul says in Galatians, but how what he says in Galatians compares with what is written about him in the book of Acts. If we take the narrative of Acts at face value, where do we see Paul visit Galatia? Luke says Paul visits the "region of Phrygia and Galatia" twice (Acts 16:6; 18:23), during his second and third journeys respectively. For centuries,

9. DeMaris, "Water Ritual," 405.

scholars thought that Galatia referred to the north-central portion of Anatolia. And they thought this for good reason because over time the provincial lines were redrawn again and again. By the end of the 3rd century (297 CE), the later and smaller size of Galatia in the north became the standard way that people thought of it afterwards.[10]

An example that comes to mind about how we often import contemporary maps onto earlier periods in history (and there's so many examples of this), is how the Latter-day Saints (LDS), or Mormons, first arrived in Utah. In November 1846, they left western Illinois and traveled through Iowa, Nebraska, and Wyoming, until they finally settled in Utah on July 24, 1847. And yet, only Illinois was officially a US State at the time (1818). As this example shows, it's easy to misspeak about geographical areas when we subsequently come to call those places by different names or draw new lines around them.

In the time of Paul, the Roman province of Galatia was actually much bigger than north-central Anatolia. When the province was originally created by Caesar Augustus in 25 BCE, it extended far enough south to include the cities mentioned in Paul's first missionary journey recorded in Acts 13–14 (Lystra, Derbe, Pisidian Antioch, and Iconium). Although Luke does not mention the province of "Galatia" explicitly when he reports Paul's first missionary journey, Paul could have gone through south Galatia three times, once per journey. When Paul travels through "Galatia" on his second and third journeys, as Luke says without reference to any cities in the province, he may have visited the same portion of Galatia as in his first journey. What makes this likely is that Acts 18:23 mentions that Paul was "strengthening all the disciples" in the region of Galatia during his third missionary journey, and yet Acts

10. Longenecker, *Galatians*, lxiii.

16:6 makes no mention of Paul doing any ministry in Galatia, only travel, during his second missionary journey.[11] Furthermore, the only other place where Luke brings together the Greek words for "strengthening" (*epistērizo*) and "disciples" (*mathētēs*) as he does in Acts 18:23 is when he records Paul's activity in Lystra, Iconium, and Antioch during his first missionary journey (Acts 14:22).

Archeologically, the evidence also suggests that Paul would never have traveled to the northern part of the province. Notably, the cities mentioned in Acts 13–14 were originally veteran colonies united by the *Via Sebaste* in 6 BCE,[12] and there were no paved road systems in the north until 80 CE.[13] In fact, Stephen Mitchell, who wrote the standard study on ancient Anatolia, said that, after surveying the archeological evidence for this debate, "There is virtually nothing to be said for the north Galatian theory."[14] Those who know the topography, geography, and archeology of ancient Turkey (Türkiye) best, affirm the south Galatia hypothesis.

An objection to the south Galatia view is that ethnic Galatians from Gaul primarily lived in the northern part of the province, and thus it would be strange for Paul to address other ethnicities with the label "Galatians." But it is probably best to think that the ethnic diversity of the south explains why Paul would use a *provincial* title to refer to his recipients. Corinthians are from Corinth, Romans are from Rome, and Philippians are from Philippi, but what do you call people from Pisidian Antioch, Lystra, Derbe, *and*

---

11. Hansen, "Galatia," 379.
12. Hansen, "Galatia," 384.
13. See French, "Acts and the Roman Roads," 56.
14. Mitchell, *Anatolia*, 2:3.

Iconium? "Galatians" is the legal title that they would have in common.[15]

WHEN DID PAUL WRITE TO SOUTH GALATIA?

The main question about when Galatians was written, if we can assume a south Galatia destination, is whether Paul's trip to Jerusalem in Gal 2:1–10 is the same trip as the so-called Jerusalem Council that Luke depicts in Acts 15. How you answer this has the biggest impact on dating the letter. Most scholars think these accounts refer to the same event. And while there are a lot of good reasons to think this, one of the problems with this view is that, according to Acts, Paul goes off to south-central Anatolia (i.e., Lystra, Derbe, Iconium, and Pisidian Antioch) *before the council* in Acts 15, yet in the autobiography of Galatians 1–2, Paul never mentions going any further away from Jerusalem than Cilicia, which is just north of Syria. Perhaps Paul was not trying to provide an exhaustive itinerary of his travels, and maybe he left out further travels.

Let's think about this though. It would be strange for Paul to leave out of the sequence of events a time period in which he visited the people to whom he was writing if it occurred in that same general period. It's also not likely that Paul would omit that he traveled *further away* from Jerusalem, because one of the emphases of the autobiography is that he spent so little time in Jerusalem and was in fact mostly very far away from it. It would only help his argument if he went to south-central Anatolia.[16] The Paul who is so eager to stress his geographical distance from

15. Ramsay, *Historical Commentary*, 312–13.

16. Or even further to the Aegean, as Campbell argues (*Framing Paul*, 190–253), contending that Paul wrote 1 Thessalonians in the late 30s CE.

Jerusalem, even to the point of swearing an oath about it (Gal 1:20), would not fail to score that point. It seems to me, then, that either Acts 13–14 is a fabrication, or the events in Gal 2:1–10 precede those recorded in Acts 13–14.

So which Jerusalem visit recorded in Acts would Gal 2:1–10 line up with? If you compare the sequence of visits that Paul makes to Jerusalem in Acts 9–15 with Galatians 1–2, the answer is clear. In Galatians, Paul only records two different visits to Jerusalem. Note the following:

1. Paul visits Peter and James in Jerusalem for fifteen-days after his transformative calling (Gal 1:18–19)

2. Paul returns to Jerusalem for a *private* meeting with the "pillar apostles" in which Paul was inspired by a "revelation" to confirm whether he was spinning his wheels, so to speak, and they gave him "the right arm of fellowship" and told him to "remember the poor" (Gal 2:1–10)

In Acts, Paul visits Jerusalem three times throughout Acts 9–15. Note the following:

1. Paul appears in Jerusalem after his calling (Acts 9:26–31)

2. Paul goes to Jerusalem for a famine relief visit inspired by the prophet Agabus (Acts 11:27–30)

3. Paul returns for the *public* Jerusalem Council regarding whether gentiles should be circumcised (Acts 15)

This means that Gal 2:1–10 could be the famine visit mentioned in Acts 11. In other words, the so-called Jerusalem Council of Acts 15 might not have happened yet at the time that Galatians was written.

One indication that this may be the case is the fact that, when Paul describes Peter's hypocrisy in Antioch of withdrawing from eating with gentiles, he adds that "even Barnabas" was led astray by this (Gal 2:13). Speaking in this way suggests that the Galatians had familiarity with him, and Acts records that Barnabas only traveled with Paul for Paul's first missionary journey. Timothy isn't mentioned in Galatians, although he is named in most other Pauline letters (minus Ephesians and Titus), and he joins Paul for his second missionary journey from Lystra in Acts 16 after the Jerusalem Council.

What could also suggest that the Jerusalem Council had not yet occurred when Galatians was written is not only the fact that the letter addresses the same topic as the Council, but also that Paul never seems to reference more than one visit to Galatia. If Paul wrote Galatians after his second or third missionary journeys, then we might expect the letter to mention that he visited them multiple times. The only place where it might is Gal 4:13. This is where Paul says that he "formerly" preached the gospel to them because of a "weakness of the flesh." That word "formerly" in Greek (*proteron*) could be rendered as "the first time." This would then mean that Paul had visited them more than once. What makes "the first time" an unlikely translation, though, is the fact that nowhere else in Galatians does Paul describe anything other than an initial encounter with them. If Acts is a helpful guide for understanding Paul's ministry, as I take it to be, then it seems best that Paul wrote Galatians between his first and second missionary journey, even if he wrote shortly after the Jerusalem Council and refers to it in Galatians 2.

As Paul also says in his letter, the Galatians have turned away from his initial proclamation "so quickly" (Gal 1:6), implying a relatively recent departure, though this is not conclusive evidence on its own, because the Galatians could merely have turned "so quickly" after being introduced to the aberrant teaching.[17] But in light of the other evidence just marshalled, I do think their turn away "so quickly" could imply that he was just with them not too long ago.

LUKE'S DESCRIPTION OF PAUL'S INITIAL MINISTRY IN GALATIA

If Paul wrote to south Galatia, regardless of *when* he wrote to them, what do we learn about Paul's ministry from Acts 13–14? What parallels might we find with Paul's brief references to that ministry in Gal 3:1–5 and 4:12–20, and to his brief allusions elsewhere in the letter?

According to Acts, Paul and Barnabas had a rough go in south Galatia. In Pisidian Antioch, they taught about Jesus with reference to Israelite history and prophetic expectation of a regal figure in the line of David whom God raised from the dead and now offers justification to those who believe (Acts 13:16–41). Afterwards, some of the Jewish people there "were filled with zeal" (Acts 13:45) and they stirred up other prominent locals to help expel them from the city (Acts 13:50). In the midst of this turmoil, Paul connects his experience to the vocation of the Servant of Isaiah, citing Isa 49:6 about being a light to the gentiles (Acts 13:47). After this they went to Iconium, where some of the Jewish people similarly incited townspeople against Paul and Barnabas (Acts 14:2) even though their teaching was accompanied by signs and wonders (Acts 14:3). Once Paul and Barnabas heard of a plot to mistreat and stone them (Acts 14:5), they fled to Lystra, Derbe, and surrounding areas (Acts 14:6–7). While they were in Lystra, they performed miracles and were believed to be gods in human form (Acts 14:8–18), which frustrated the Jews from Antioch and Iconium who followed them there. These people

17. Silva, *Interpreting Galatians*, 139n19.

won enough of the crowd over to their side to then stone Paul and drag him outside the city to be left for dead (Acts 14:19). Surviving this incident, Paul and Barnabas went to Derbe from there, and then they returned through the same cities "strengthening the disciples" by reminding them "we must go through many hardships to enter the kingdom of God" (Acts 14:22).

As this summary indicates, Acts 13–14 describes how Paul was physically harmed during his first missionary journey such that he was nearly stoned to death (cf. 2 Tim 3:11). Paul does not mention being stoned in Galatians, but he does in 2 Cor 11:25, which is possibly a reference to this hardship in south Galatia recorded in Acts.[18] I contend that this record in Acts provides the best evidence for what Paul's "weakness of the flesh" actually was, not least given how Acts seems to hint at how Paul's travels were disrupted by this stoning. Thus, suffering itself provides another bit of evidence that Galatians was written to the south of the province, although proponents of the south Galatia theory don't acknowledge this point.[19]

What this could then suggest is that "the marks of Jesus" to which Paul appeals to conclude his letter (Gal 6:17) are not physical manifestations of any type of suffering or persecution that he may have endured, but specifically those that he received when he was ministering among them in Galatia. These marks that the Galatians once recognized as revealing Christ to them have sometime subsequently turned into a source of derision, which is the topic for our time next chapter.

---

18. Pobee, *Persecution and Martyrdom*, 95.
19. Cf., e.g., Longenecker, *Galatians*, lxix.

CONCLUDING THOUGHTS

Paul's initial ministry in Galatia was characterized by hardship (cf. Acts 13–14). He experienced a "weakness of the flesh," which may have been the result of stoning and other ill-treatment, that impacted his travel plans and was the occasion for his initial proclamation of the good news (Gal 4:13). Paul reminds them of snippets of that message in Galatians, including the story of his transformation and how vices hinder inheriting the kingdom (Gal 1:13–14; 5:19–21; cf. 1:8–9). In the light of relevance theory, we can assume that Paul's initial ministry in Galatia also included performing the ritual of baptism (Gal 3:26–29; cf. 4:19) and addressing the topics of suffering (cf. Acts 14:22) as well as caring for the poor (Gal 2:10; cf. 1 Cor 16:1–4). Undoubtedly, there was plenty more that Paul said and did, as relevance theory reminds us and as Acts 13–14 supports. As Paul proclaimed the gospel in that weakened state of suffering (Gal 4:13), he portrayed Christ crucified to the Galatians (cf. Gal 3:1), and indeed they welcomed him into their community as if he was Christ himself (Gal 4:14). But after he left Galatia things changed, and they did so quickly.

REFLECTIONS

1. Thinking about relevance theory some more, are there any other teachings that you think were likely part of Paul's initial proclamation to the Galatians? Why?

2. How much weight do you think we should give to Acts for reconstructing Paul's ministry in Galatia, given the debate about the destination of the letter?

4

AFTER PAUL LEFT GALATIA

AFTER PAUL LEFT GALATIA, the relationship he had established with the Galatians deteriorated. But what caused things to change, or better, *who* caused things to change, and to do so "so quickly"? As Paul says in his rebuke:

> **Gal 1:6-7:** I marvel that you are turning so quickly from the one who called you in the grace of Christ to another gospel, which is not another, except some are troubling you and wishing to tweak the gospel of Christ.

Paul refers to a group of unnamed "troublemakers" as the source of the crisis and he expresses his concerns that they bear a false gospel. What else can we learn about this group of troublemakers from the letter and their sudden influence in Galatia after Paul left? Who were they, where did they come from, what were they teaching, and how were they going about things? In order to answer these questions about what happened in the (recent) *past*, we have to disentangle this from what Paul says about the *present* crisis.

Since Paul's response to the crisis is technically the focus of chapters 5–7 of the present book, we have to try to tease out *what happened* versus how Paul may be interpreting *what is taking place*. We have to sift through Paul's polemics against his opponents in order to glean what we can about what they have been saying and doing in his absence. This is a notoriously difficult task, but it is a necessary one.

MIRROR-READING

Since all of Galatians is occasioned by the crisis, we should assume that what Paul addresses in the letter is prompted by the situation. If, for example, the troublemakers were accusing Paul of something, whatever it may be, the fact that they were doing so and the nature of that accusation is crucial for us to try to discern in this chapter. But it must be acknowledged that we only have access to such a hypothetical accusation through Paul's response. Again, this makes the investigation fraught with difficulties. But this is where it is helpful to discuss the topic of mirror-reading.

Mirror-reading is a tool that we use to think about why a person says what they say in the context of an argument. As the name implies, we use the text as a mirror, so to speak, to try and discern how it might *reflect* what the other side of the dispute is saying. As an illustration, let's recall the speech from *Independence Day* once more. By way of mirror-reading, it is clear that the threat aims at destroying all of humanity, even though we never hear their side of the story. This seems simple enough, but mirror-reading can be abused and overdone, not least because polemics are so commonly full of distortions, as is terribly apparent from contemporary political discourse. New Testament scholar, John M. G. Barclay, wrote a famous article on the topic of mirror-reading and used Galatians as a test case, applying a chastened version of it to make conclusions about the crisis on a spectrum of certain (or virtually certain), highly probable, probable, possible, conceivable, and incredible.[1] Barclay's work on mirror-reading reminds us to acknowledge its limitations and distortions up front, even while recognizing that mirror-reading is inevitable.[2]

Another illustration that gets at the tension inherent in mirror-reading can be found in a modern polemical letter. The letter that I have in mind was an open letter written in 2010 by Dan Gilbert, the owner of the NBA basketball team, the Cleveland Cavaliers, which he wrote to the city of Cleveland and fans of the franchise in response to superstar LeBron James's choice to leave the team for the Miami Heat during a special televised program on ESPN called *The Decision*.[3] (For context, this was the first time LeBron left the franchise; he later returned for four seasons in 2014–2018 and helped them win an NBA title in 2016, before joining the Los Angeles Lakers in 2018.) Given the nature of LeBron's "decision" to leave Cleveland the first time, Dan Gilbert had a lot of things to say. He maligned LeBron for his "narcissism" and "betrayal," and promised Cavs fans that this would only motivate the organization further to win a title in his absence. Thinking about this letter in terms of mirror-reading, it is clear that at times Gilbert conveys things that LeBron said and did, but even so it is laced with polemical distortion. At other times in the letter, Gilbert puts words in LeBron's mouth to convey how he (Gilbert) viewed LeBron, not how LeBron viewed himself or the situation. For example, Gilbert writes: "Some people think they

1. Barclay, "Mirror-Reading."
2. Though see Hardin, "Galatians 1–2 Without A Mirror."
3. Gilbert's open letter is no longer published on the Cleveland Cavaliers website, but other news outlets reposted the letter in its entirety. See, e.g., https://www.espn.com/nba/news/story?id=5365704

should go to heaven but NOT have to die to get there. Sorry, but that's simply not how it works." Was LeBron attempting to go to heaven without dying? We would be led astray by Gilbert's polemics if we used mirror-reading to conclude that LeBron actually believed this. Gilbert is suggesting that by leaving for Miami, LeBron wants to take the easy path to a championship. Often people will distort what their enemies say or think in the heat of an argument by taking their opponent's views to logical extremes, and the (Miami) Heat was clearly getting to Gilbert.

It should also be acknowledged that it is much easier to sift through the polemics of a modern letter, like we just did, about a topic that received a great deal of media attention, than an ancient letter. Indeed, it is much more difficult to try to understand a crisis when we not only have one side of the conversation, as we have acknowledged many times, but specifically *one side of an argument*, and a highly polemical one at that. Mirror-reading is an exegetical tool to help with this problem, but sometimes it is not the right tool for the job. We need to be careful and cautious about how and when we deploy it.

SHUT OUT BY ZEALOUS TROUBLEMAKERS

When we turn now to look at what we can gather from Galatians about what transpired since the time Paul left Galatia, the best place to start is with those passages that mention Paul's ministry in Gal 4:12–20 and 3:1–5. This is where I began the last chapter, but I stopped halfway through each passage because Paul's attention shifts from his initial encounter to the influence of these troublemakers. We can now look at what the second half of each passage reveals, beginning with Gal 4:12–20:

> **Gal 4:15-20:** Where then is your blessing? For I testify to you that, if possible, you would have gouged out your eyes and given them to me. So then, have I become your enemy by telling the truth to you? They are zealous for you, not in a good way, but they want to shut you out, in order that you might be zealous for them. Now, it is always good to be zealous[4] for a good reason, and not only when I am present with you. My children, for whom again I have birth pains until Christ might be formed in you. I would like to be present with you now and change my tone, because I am perplexed by you.

The mutuality and reciprocity that Paul experienced with the Galatians when he was dealing with his weakness has gone away. The Galatians have abandoned that blessing, and have now become closer to enemies, and Paul is experiencing prolonged birth pains, as it were, waiting for the full formation of Christ within them that began when he was first there.

All of this disruption is due to the influence of those troublemakers. Paul does not mention them overtly, but he does refer to them when he says,

> **Gal 4:17:** *They* are zealous for you, not in a good way, but *they* want to shut you out, in order that you might be zealous for *them*.

Paul characterizes the actions of the troublemakers as "zealous," but he qualifies this by adding that it is not a good kind of zeal. Instead, they are "shutting out" the Galatians. Presumably this refers to some kind of ostracization, excluding uncircumcised male gentiles from full participation in the community as leverage so that the Galatians do what the

---

4. I take the infinitive as middle in voice rather than passive. Cf. also HCSB; NIV.

troublemakers want. To be sure, zeal isn't a bad thing in itself (Gal 4:18), but the troublemakers are not displaying the good kind, which Paul knows something about, given how zeal led him to persecute the church of God (Gal 1:13–14).

SUFFERING OVER CIRCUMCISION

In Gal 3:1–5, Paul also shifts in the second half of the passage to touch on aspects of the present crisis, though here it is much less direct.

> **Gal 3:3–5:** Are you foolish like this: beginning by the Spirit are you now perfected by the flesh? Did you suffer so much in vain? If indeed it was in vain. Does the one who supplies the Spirit to you and works miracles among you, do so by works of the law or by hearing with faith?

Paul oscillates from the Galatians' initial reception of the Spirit when he was with them (Gal 3:2), to the way that they are now aiming to be perfected by the flesh (Gal 3:3), as Paul characterizes it. Given that the central issue of this letter is whether the gentile men in Galatia ought to be circumcised, we should understand "flesh" here as a way of referring to the procedure of circumcision. This kind of shorthand works because circumcision is fundamentally a removal of flesh from the flesh. Once Paul brings up the flesh, with its connotations of the present crisis surrounding circumcision, he then asks if they "suffered" so many things in vain (Gal 3:4). Some scholars have thought that this is an odd question in a context about the reception of the Spirit, and so they translate the Greek verb *paschō* differently so that Paul instead asks them if they "experienced" so much in vain, referring to their positive spiritual experiences.[5]

---

5. English translations are divided on this verse. For "experience"

But, as we saw in the last chapter, the context of the passage begins with Paul mentioning his own suffering as he proclaimed the good news about the crucified Messiah (Gal 3:1). So, a question about the suffering of the Galatians is hardly out of left field. And since Paul has just asked about the present crisis of circumcision by mentioning the flesh (Gal 3:3), the notion of suffering is best understood as relating to the conditions in which circumcision has become a pressing issue for them.[6] Indeed, when we compare how Gal 3:1–5 shifts from Paul's initial ministry to the present crisis with a question about suffering, it parallels how Paul transitions to describe how the troublemakers are "shutting out" the Galatians with their zeal in Gal 4:12–20. In other words, the suffering of Gal 3:4 most likely relates to the kind of social ostracization that Paul mentions in 4:17.

Paul concludes this section by saying that God continues to supply the Spirit to them within the present crisis (Gal 3:5), and he does so on the same basis as he did when they first received the Spirit (Gal 3:2). Neither their lack of circumcision nor the presence of suffering means that God has abandoned them. Paul adds that the Spirit works "miracles" among them, which could refer to any number of powerful signs, but likely includes, given the contextual references to suffering, acts of healing and empowerment in the midst of their own weakness, as they struggle to stand firm in the present crisis.

---

see, e.g., NIV; NLT; NRSVue. For "suffer" see, e.g., ESV; HCSB; KJV; NASB; NET.

6. For a fuller defense, see Dunne, "Suffering in Vain"; idem, *Persecution and Participation*, 69–78.

CIRCUMCISION & COERCION

Reminding ourselves of the pitfalls of mirror-reading, it is possible that Paul has distorted what the troublemakers were doing in Galatia. Our first attempt at determining whether or not he has twisted things, though, should be to ensure that we are at least seeing the full picture that he is painting. That picture may be distorted, but it is still important to acknowledge how Paul wants his readers to see things. It may be that his depictions are accurate, but we need to keep gleaning what we can before we determine that.

There are a few other passages in the letter where we find other overt references to Paul's opponents that we will turn to now, including Gal 5:7–12 and 6:12–13.

> **Gal 5:7–12:** You were running well; who hindered you from obeying the truth? This persuasion is not from the one calling you. A little leaven leavens the whole lump. I am persuaded about you in the Lord that you will think no other thing, and the one troubling you will bear the judgment, whoever he might be. And I, siblings, if I still preach circumcision, why am I still being persecuted? Then the scandal of the cross is nullified. I wish that those agitating you would emasculate themselves!

In this passage, Paul speaks of his opponents in terms of "troublemaking" once more, but now adds the term "agitating." Both of these terms continue to speak to the distress and harm that they were causing the community. We also learn from this passage that the troublemakers have been influential, which Paul characterizes as impeding runners in a race and as leaven spreading throughout a lump of dough.

Turning to Gal 6:12–13, the final passage that overtly mentions Paul's opponents, we read:

> **Gal 6:12–13:** As many as want to put on a good show in the flesh, these compel you to be circumcised, only in order that they might not be persecuted for the cross of Christ. For not even those who are circumcised keep the law, but they want you to be circumcised, in order that they might boast in your flesh.

From this passage we see very clearly that Paul's opponents want the gentile men in Galatia to be circumcised. Paul characterizes this as a desire to "put on a good show in the flesh" and to "boast in your flesh." The link between circumcision and the flesh is made plain, highlighting how circumcision is implied earlier in the letter when Paul asked if the Galatians were now being perfected in the flesh (Gal 3:3). As we will see, this connection is part of Paul's polemics at key points in the letter as he associates his opponents with the flesh over and against the Spirit.

Paul adds in Gal 6:12–13 that his opponents are circumcised, which most scholars take as indicating that they were Jewish, though some suggest that these figures have undergone the procedure of circumcision as adults. This would make them gentiles who underwent full proselyte conversion to Judaism. Since Paul also says that they do not "keep the law" in context, this could be a jab at their lack of understanding of the law in some way. We will have more to say about what Paul's polemical accusation that they do not "keep the law" means in chapter 7, but for our purposes here it is worth stating that the argument that Paul's opponents were former gentiles fails to convince. A good comparison is Paul's reference to "those from the circumcision" in Jerusalem, or as some earlier interpreters rendered the phrase, "the circumcision party." The presence of this group is what caused Peter to withdraw from eating with gentiles (Gal 2:12), but there the reference to circumcision does not refer to adult converts to Judaism. If that is what was meant by "the circumcision party," that would incidentally make it the one party that you don't want to get invited to! But in all seriousness, just as that label "those from the circumcision" designates those who are already circumcised, and simply refers to a group of Jewish people, the same appears to be true here in Gal 6:13 for the troublemakers when Paul refers to "those who are circumcised." I contend that he gives them this designation because of their outsized view of circumcision as something worth boasting in over and against the cross.

Paul also seems to be conveying that the troublemakers are not merely promoting circumcision by persuasion, as if "compelling" the Galatians to be circumcised means that the troublemakers simply have really good arguments. Outside of the Jewish world, Paula Fredriksen notes, circumcision was "a disgusting self-mutilation" and "a custom … fit only for derision."[7] To be sure, we do know of Anatolian practices of male genital mutilation, such as those associated with the priests of Cybele, but this was by no means a widespread practice, and it may have been the case that the cult was a haven for eunuchs and others who were already castrated.[8] Given that circumcision was a painful procedure to a very sensitive area of the body, we have to stop and think about why grown gentile men would want to go forward with this. After all, there's a reason why the Jewish custom is to perform this procedure when a baby boy is eight days old. So, when Paul refers to the actions of the troublemakers as "compulsion," this likely speaks to

7. Fredriksen, *Paul*, 43. See also Soon, "The Bestial Glans"; idem, *A Disabled Apostle*, 82–128.

8. Bowden, *Mystery Cults*, 104, cf. 96–104.

how they are *forcing* the Galatians to be circumcised, which matches how they are "shutting them out" from the community (Gal 4:17), and agitating and troubling them as they suffer with this decision (Gal 3:4; cf. 1:8–9; 5:10–12). The rationale behind why the troublemakers would insist so much, even to the point of causing harm, is suggested by the motivation that Paul ascribes to them with respect to avoiding persecution "for the cross of Christ" (which incidentally suggests that they were Christ-followers too). Paul does not say who might be doing this persecution or why, but his words suggest that if the Galatians receive circumcision, Paul's opponents themselves would no longer experience persecution. It seems then that Paul imagines a three-tiered crisis: pressure upon the troublemakers in turn leads them to pressure the Galatians. If the Galatians simply receive circumcision, it will all go away. Since Paul does not say more about the nature of this three-tiered crisis, we don't need to give an explanation *for his explanation*. But if we did want to attempt to offer one, we will need to go beyond the letter and think more about the setting of the province of Galatia itself, building upon our conclusions from the previous chapter.

WHO WAS PRESSURING THE TROUBLEMAKERS?

Most likely the unnamed group placing pressure on the troublemakers was either the local synagogue, local civic officials, or some combination of them.[9] Intriguingly, Luke's account of the hostility that Paul experienced in Acts 13–14 was fomented by some "zealous" Jews, people of prominent position, and other local townspeople, and it may be that

9. Zealots in Jerusalem have also been suggested, but this only works if (a) the troublemakers were from Jerusalem, and (b) the Zealots cared about gentile proselytes in the diaspora.

the conditions that Luke describes persisted or worsened after Paul left. Regardless, it seems most likely to me that the influence of the Roman Empire was the greatest contributing factor here. Even if the local synagogue was part of the picture, Roman influence would best explain their concern about gentile circumcision as well.

In the previous chapter, I argued that Paul likely wrote to churches in south Galatia: Pisidian Antioch, Lystra, Derbe, and Iconium. In Roman Galatia as a whole, Roman imperialism was pervasive, including in these four cities. Derbe and Iconium, for example, were both titled Claudioderbe and Claudiconium respectively during the reign of Claudius (41–54 CE),[10] and Pisidian Antioch and Lystra were originally founded by Augustus as colonies established for veteran soldiers of the Roman Empire in 25 BCE.

Pisidian Antioch, in particular, was meant to be an alternate Rome within Asia Minor.[11] As a town full of military vets, there would have been a strong degree of patriotism, and as Alison Cooley states, these figures would have been "entrusted with the task of securing Rome's grip on its newly annexed territory."[12] Pisidian Antioch even had a prominent imperial temple dedicated to Augustus at the top of the town, which was most likely in use prior to Augustus's death in 14 CE.[13] Just outside the entry to the temple there was a prominent inscription known as the *Res Gestae Divi Augusti*, which functioned like a public résumé cataloguing the great accomplishments of Caesar Augustus. This inscription was written in Latin, further highlighting just how strong the Roman presence was in the city. Evidence

---

10. M. Wilson, *Biblical Turkey*, 158.
11. Cooley, *Res Gestae*, 14.
12. Cooley, *Res Gestae*, 240.
13. Mitchell and Waelkens, *Pisidian Antioch*, 167.

of the inscription survives in 270 fragments,[14] but an inscription was also found further north in the province near Ancyra (in both Latin and Greek). Outside of Asia Minor (and, more specifically, Roman Galatia), evidence of the inscription was only found in Apollonia (in Greek). Cooley contends that, given the lack of widespread evidence of the inscription, it was likely not an empire-wide commission, but rather a provincial one. This could suggest a distinctive imperial influence on the whole of Roman Galatia relative to the rest of Asia Minor.

The significance of highlighting the influence of Roman ideology in the cities of south Galatia is how it could have factored into what made circumcision such a pressing issue. As we saw in chapter 2 with the counter-imperial readings of Galatians, circumcision could provide the legal coverage for gentile men who have come to reject their former beliefs as they turned to Christ, but who would still be required to perform their civic duties in honor of the gods and Caesar. Unless they received circumcision and belonged to Judaism, gentiles would be in a precarious space without legal protection for their newfound convictions.[15]

I find local imperial influence, in broad brush strokes, to be the most likely explanation for Paul's reference to those persecuting the troublemakers in Gal 6:12. Fascinatingly, this is a view that goes as far back as St. Jerome at least (mid fourth–early fifth century CE). He summarizes this interpretation quite succinctly in his commentary on Gal 6:12, and so it is worth citing in full:

> Gaius [Julius] Caesar, Octavian Augustus, and Augustus's successor Tiberius had published laws that allowed the Jews scattered throughout the whole stretch of the Roman Empire to live by

14. Cooley, *Res Gestae*, 14.
15. See especially Hardin, *Galatians*.

> their own rites and to keep their ancestral ceremonies. Therefore, whoever was circumcised, even if he was a Christian, was considered a Jew by outsiders. But anyone who was not circumcised, and by his uncircumcision declared that he was not a Jew, became liable to persecution from Gentile and Jew alike. Those who had led the Galatians astray were hoping to evade persecution and persuaded the disciples to be circumcised for protection. The Apostle now says they put their trust in the flesh because they made circumcision a matter worthy of persecution for both the Gentiles, whom they feared, and the Jews, whom they wanted to please. For neither the Jews nor the Gentiles could persecute people they saw circumcising new converts and keeping the commandments of the Law.[16]

This dynamic is, I think, quite right. But to be clear, though, this does not mean that Rome is the foil for what Paul says. He is not arguing against Roman ideology in Galatians. Furthermore, this background does not rule out the fact that the broader societal conflict suggested by Gal 6:12 also includes a confluence of multiple groups, including local leaders from the synagogue or even disgruntled family members at home. It also does not mean that there was any systematic persecution of Christ-followers by Roman officials. This proposal simply suggests that local Roman imperialism provides one important social and political factor for what made the crisis so pressing.

---

16. St. Jerome, *Commentary on Galatians*, 262–63.

SUBTLE CLUES ABOUT THE TEACHING OF THE TROUBLEMAKERS

There are a few other passages in Galatians where, although the troublemakers are not mentioned overtly, we can probably glean more about their teaching and tactics based on mirror-reading. First off, what were they likely saying about Paul? Given that Paul offers a unique autobiographical summary of his transformation and traveling ministry, it raises the question about whether some of the information that he reports has been reported differently. Paul does not offer the same kind of overview anywhere else, which is suggestive. But furthermore, Paul is not merely reporting information for the sake of it. We won't get into the specifics just yet, because that is technically part of how Paul responds to the crisis in Galatia (cf. chapter 5), but here we get the impression that Paul challenges how his story is being told. Paul emphasizes that he did not spend much time in Jerusalem nor much time with the Jerusalem apostles shortly after his transformation. When we connect that emphasis with Paul's opening qualification of his apostleship as not being derivative, but instead directly given to him by divine appointment (Gal 1:1), just as his gospel was as well (Gal 1:11–12), it is possible that the troublemakers were claiming that Paul's authority is secondary to the authority of the Jerusalem apostles. It would be difficult to say definitively what the troublemakers were saying about Paul's relationship to Jerusalem exactly, and how that related to the authenticity of his gospel and his apostleship, but it seems likely that Paul chose to tell these features of his story in part because of something the troublemakers were saying about it.

In two different instances Paul seems to directly address accusations made against him by the troublemakers based on rhetorical questions that he asks the Galatians. The assumption here is that Paul is likely not asking these questions out of the blue, but is instead raising these issues because people are talking about them. The first one is in Gal 1:10.

> **Gal 1:10:** For do I now persuade people or God? Or do I seek to please people? If I am still pleasing people, I would not be a slave of the Messiah.

Here Paul asks two rhetorical questions, both of which are dense. Whatever prompted the questions, Paul insists that he is not a people pleaser, but a slave of the Messiah.[17] In the light of the issues of circumcision in the letter, it seems that Paul's emphasis on being a slave of the Messiah rather than a people pleaser relates to his commitment to Christ regardless of whatever hardships he may face. If the troublemakers were claiming the opposite, that Paul was a people pleaser, then it would make sense that he is here rejecting that designation. Being a people pleaser, in the light of the crisis, would then likely mean that Paul's circumcision-free gospel for the gentiles aims at pleasing people rather than fidelity to God, since it won't demand a painful procedure for converts. Whether or not the troublemakers were claiming that Paul was a people pleaser, Paul wants to be clear that he wasn't one.

The other rhetorical question that could arise from one of the troublemakers' accusations is found in Gal 5:11.

> **Gal 5:11:** Siblings, if I still preach circumcision, why am I still being persecuted? Then the scandal of the cross is nullified.

---

17. This probably explains that he is also not trying to "persuade" people either, and so he is trying to persuade/please God. Cf. 1 Thess 2:4–5.

This rhetorical question could be prompted by the troublemakers claiming the opposite, that Paul continues to preach circumcision. But if that were the case, what would be the point of Paul insisting that he's not a people pleaser? Were the troublemakers saying that he is a people pleaser by leaving out circumcision, or that he actually does continue to preach circumcision and just failed to mention it to the Galatians? Perhaps the troublemakers didn't actually claim either of these things about Paul and he is just responding to two different hypothetical objections to his circumcision-free gospel. Perhaps the seeming incompatibility of these claims should suggest to us that the troublemakers weren't claiming just one thing about Paul as if they spoke with one voice. In other words, maybe there was general confusion about Paul's circumcision-free gospel, with some claiming that Paul left it out because he was a people pleaser and others claiming that he actually continues to advocate circumcision for all followers of Jesus.

It's not clear exactly what the troublemakers were claiming about Paul based upon the potential accusations in Gal 1:10 and 5:11, or the fact that Paul feels a strong need to narrate key events from his life in the autobiography. It's also not clear if the troublemakers were claiming the same thing. But a modest use of mirror-reading suggests that Paul believed that the legitimacy of his circumcision-free gospel, and thus his apostolic authority by extension, was being questioned to some degree.

What else were the troublemakers teaching? Of course, the corollary of Paul's circumcision-free gospel for the gentiles suggests that Paul's opponents were teaching something about circumcision. It is fairly likely that biblical injunctions to receive circumcision were part of their message. The most crucial of these, especially given Paul's appeal to Abraham at key points in the argument, was likely Genesis 17, where circumcision is first mentioned in the Torah and incorporated as a crucial commandment in the covenant that God made with Abraham. We might be able to say more about the teaching of the troublemakers through the method of mirror-reading, and we should assume that there was more, but I am not too confident about saying much more myself. So, Paul's opponents were likely teaching about circumcision and calling Paul's gospel and/or apostleship into question, but what can we discern about their tactics?

SUBTLE CLUES ABOUT THE TACTICS OF THE TROUBLEMAKERS

As we have already seen, the effect of the troublemakers' insistence on circumcision seems to have created communal tension in Paul's absence. Paul's letter suggests that the troublemakers were forcing the gentile men to be circumcised, and they were zealously "shutting out" the gentiles until they did so. The turmoil related to this seems to be reflected in a few other places in Galatians where Paul does not overtly mention the troublemakers, but given the way he has associated them with the flesh, he seems to be further acknowledging the division that they were causing.

At the end of the famous allegory of Galatians 4, Paul says, "But just as then the one born according to the flesh persecuted the one born according to the Spirit, so also it is now" (Gal 4:29). What is happening "now" is our concern in this chapter: people associated with the flesh were persecuting people associated with the Spirit. Undoubtedly, this comment speaks to matters that go beyond the present crisis in Galatia, but it would be a mistake to miss how it also includes that crisis. This verse adds corroborating evidence that Paul's opponents were creating serious problems for the communities in Galatia through their insistence on circumcision.

This association between the flesh and social disruption is also suggested in two other passages. After Paul says that the Galatians should not use their freedom as an "opportunity for the flesh" (Gal 5:13), which in context ought to include circumcision and the social division that it creates, he reminds them of the importance of loving one another as the fulfillment of the law (Gal 5:14). He then adds: "But if you bite and devour one another, beware lest you are consumed by one another" (Gal 5:15). The matter of circumcision—this "opportunity for the flesh"—is leading to the kinds of social turmoil that would be expected by ravenous animals, not siblings who ought to love each other.

Second, and finally, Paul also seems to allude to the tactics of the troublemakers when he lists the "works of the flesh" just a few verses later.

> **Gal 5:19-21:** Now the works of the flesh are revealed, which are sexual immorality, impurity, sensuality, idolatry, sorcery, hostilities, strife, zeal, anger, rivalries, divisions, factions, envy, drunkenness, orgies, and things like these, which I tell you in advance, even as I told you before, that those doing such things will not inherit the kingdom of God.

Notice how the central vices in this list relate to matters of communal division. The works of the flesh are thus being manifested by those aligned with the flesh. This includes the *zeal* that they display as they "shut out" the Galatians (Gal 4:17), and even the "sorcery" that they have utilized to "bewitch" the Galatians (Gal 3:1).[18] These vices, of course,

18. This is probably just an example of polemical vilification, but even so, we should not miss this association with Paul's opponents.

are general moral ills that if anyone displays them they would threaten to keep them away from the kingdom of God, and the irony is that those who want to circumcise the flesh were not curtailing the impulses of the works of the flesh by means of that process, but were actually exciting the flesh to be at work in Galatia.

REFLECTING ON MIRROR-READING

Taking everything together in Paul's depiction of his opponents, it is possible that he has not described them accurately. They may have viewed the situation, themselves, and even Paul differently than he describes, but that would then raise serious doubts about Paul's rhetorical effectiveness. At the very least, Paul wants the Galatians to understand the crisis the way that he sees it, and so in order for that to be compelling, it has to cohere with their experiences. And so I assume that it does.

Based upon all of this evidence from the letter about the teaching and the tactics of Paul's opponents, I will continue to refer to them as "troublemakers" or "agitators," rather than as "Judaizers," which is the traditional designation. The reason why the former terms are preferable is because that is how Paul refers to his rivals. Paul never calls them "Judaizers," and frankly he never would have, because Judaizing is not something that Jews do, but something that non-Jews do. As has often been said in various ways, a Jew can no more Judaize than a Greek can Hellenize. Judaizing is for non-Jews just as Hellenizing is for non-Greeks. So, if the agitators were Jewish Christ-followers, as I have suggested, then the term "Judaizers" is non-sensical. On the flip side, because the terms like "troublemakers" and "agitators" are not what Paul's opponents would have called themselves, some scholars have chosen neutral language such as "the Teachers" (J. L. Martyn) or "the Influencers" (Mark Nanos). Yet, since we are trying to interpret a polemical letter, I think we should maintain Paul's polemics and use the terms that he did.

We now have a picture of what happened after Paul left Galatia. It is admittedly incomplete, and potentially distorted by Paul's polemics, but we have enough information to put together an intelligible series of events. Even though Paul did not instruct the Galatians about circumcision when he was with them (or if he did, it wasn't an emphasis), circumcision became a pressing issue because of the social displacement that the gentile men among them experienced. They were still expected to participate in local cults, and yet they believed that they had taken on a new identity relative to the local Jewish communities by embracing Paul's message about Israel's Messiah. Since these gentile men were uncircumcised, they could not be full members of the Jewish community, and they could not claim exemption from the imperial cult either. A group of Jewish Christ-followers began to insist on gentile circumcision to alleviate pressure from local civic authorities who may have viewed the Jewish communities as improperly giving cover to non-Jewish men. As a result, strife and communal division ensued, and these gentile men were being pressured to be circumcised to alleviate the tension. Once Paul heard about this, he wrote Galatians in response. It is to the heart of that response that we turn to next.

REFLECTIONS

1. Does mirror-reading seem like a helpful exegetical tool to you? Why or why not?

2. How does the socio-cultural background of the Roman Empire in Anatolia impact how you understand the Galatian crisis?

5

PAUL'S RESPONSE TO THE GALATIANS, PART ONE

Paul Is a Paradigm for Galatian Imitation

IN THE LAST TWO CHAPTERS we have seen how, when we are reading Paul's letter to the Galatians, we can partially reconstruct what happened both when Paul was in Galatia originally and shortly after he left. It is now time to make sense of how to read Paul's response to the crisis after he was informed about it over the next three chapters. Exactly how he first learned about the crisis is not entirely clear. Perhaps someone sent him a letter, but unlike the Corinthian correspondence, Paul does not refer to any kind of written communication. Regardless, he was not happy with the news that he received, and the intensity reflected in the letter likely suggests that Galatians was written shortly after Paul found out about what had been transpiring. There are at least three key threads that I think account for the heart of Paul's argument, which can help us read the letter. These are:

1. Paul is a Paradigm for Galatian Imitation
2. The Law Protected the Promise to Abraham
3. Those with the Spirit Are Above the Law

These three threads, I think, help us to organize the main points of Paul's argument for why the gentile men in Galatia do not need to receive circumcision, and, more strongly, why they should not undergo the procedure. Each of these threads will be developed over the next three chapters.

The first part of Paul's response that we need to recognize when reading Galatians is that Paul presents himself as a paradigm in the autobiography of Galatians 1–2. As noted already, Paul seems to be responding to accusations regarding his relationship to the Jerusalem apostles in the autobiography. We can't be sure what those accusations were, but the troublemakers must have said something to prompt Paul to stress the legitimacy of his apostleship and gospel (Gal 1:1, 11–12). This may also be why Paul feels the need to mention that he co-sends the letter with a group of unnamed siblings (Gal 1:2), suggesting that he has a lot of people supporting him. Paul's focus on the Jerusalem apostles is noticeable from the fact that he mentions them in each of the three subsections of the autobiography:

1. After Paul's transformation, he comments on his early days of ministry relative to his time spent in Jerusalem with Peter (called Cephas) and James (Gal 1:11–24).

2. Paul had an important encounter with the three "pillar apostles" (i.e., Peter, James, and John) on a visit to Jerusalem (Gal 2:1–10).

3. In Antioch, Peter withdrew from eating with gentiles when "people from James" arrived, and Paul confronted Peter for this (Gal 2:11–21).

In addition to addressing apparent accusations in the autobiography, Paul also seems to be pointing to himself as a paradigm for the Galatians to imitate in the present crisis.[1] What unites the whole autobiography, then, seems to be Paul's response to the (real or hypothetical) accusation that he was a people pleaser (Gal 1:10). Instead of being a people pleaser, Paul insists that he was a slave of the Messiah.

THE CALLING OF THE MESSIAH'S SLAVE (GALATIANS 1:11–24)

In the initial movement of the autobiography (Gal 1:11–24), Paul stresses that he spent little time in Jerusalem, and that he barely interacted with the apostles outside of Peter and James. Even when Paul describes how God called him away from his violent support of his ancestral traditions and revealed his Son through Paul (Gal 1:15–16b), the long sentence in Greek isn't actually completed until we get the main verbs, which stress what only seems worth stressing if these things are being disputed: "immediately I did not consult with flesh and blood, nor did I go up to Jerusalem to those who were apostles before me, but I departed to Arabia and again I returned to Damascus" (Gal 1:16c–17). In other words, Paul is saying, "I did not talk to anyone about this, nor did I go to Jerusalem, but instead went in the opposite direction." It was only three years later that he first went to Jerusalem for a short fifteen-day visit with Peter and James (Gal 1:18–19). At this point in his narration, Paul suddenly swears an oath—"Now, what I am writing to you, behold, in

1. So also, Gaventa, "Galatians 1 and 2."

the presence of God, I do not lie" (Gal 1:20). Unless there is good reason to think that Paul might be lying about this, such as his details diverging from what was being reported in Galatia, it makes no sense for Paul to swear such an oath before God. He even continues to stress this point that he went far away from Jerusalem to Syria and Cilicia (Gal 1:21), and that, although followers of Jesus in Judea knew Paul's reputation, they had no idea what he *looked like* (Gal 1:22–24).

But how do we see Paul portray himself positively as a slave of the Messiah in this first part of the autobiography? This is seen in the dramatic transformation that Paul experienced, going from a violent persecutor of Christ-followers (Gal 1:13–14) to someone who became a vital proclaimer of Christ (Gal 1:15–16). What is even more interesting here is when we look closely at how Paul describes his transformation, three times he draws from language in Isa 49:1–6 LXX,[2] where we find the servant of the LORD (or "slave").[3] Specifically, this passage is about how the servant is called to be a "light to the nations" (Isa 49:6). First, note the parallels between Gal 1:15–16 and Isa 49:1 LXX:

> **Gal 1:15–16:** But when God was pleased, the one who separated me from my mother's womb and who called me through his grace to reveal his Son through me, in order that I might proclaim the good news about him to the gentiles . . .[4]

2. Paul would have known the Hebrew Scriptures, but the evidence from his letters suggests that he often engaged the Greek translations of them commonly referred to as the Septuagint and stylized as the LXX.

3. Cf. *doulos* in Isa 49:3, 5, 7 LXX, which is the same Greek word as in Gal 1:10; although see *pais* in Isa 49:6 LXX.

4. Given Paul's close connection to the Messiah, I take the Greek phrase to mean not that God revealed his Son *to Paul*, but *through*

Isa 49:1b LXX: . . . from my mother's womb he called my name.

Being called from the womb is something of a prophetic trope (cf. Jer 1:5), but there are other allusions to Isaiah 49 in this context. Note the next example:

Gal 1:24: They glorified God because of me.

Isa 49:3 LXX: He said to me, "You are my servant (*doulos*), Israel, and in you I will be glorified."

Paul seems to interpret people glorifying God for his own transformation as being pre-figured in the glory that Isaiah's servant would bring to God. The servant is here called "Israel" because the servant is a part of Israel and represents the whole. Paul most likely believed that Jesus was *the ultimate representative servant*, but Jesus's ministry did not cease with his death. By means of his Spirit, Jesus's ministry continues on *through Paul* (cf. Gal 1:15–16; 2:19–20).

There is one final allusion to Isaiah 49 at the very beginning of the second portion of the autobiography. Paul went to Jerusalem again *fourteen years later* (Gal 2:1) for a consultation with the "pillar apostles." He quickly adds that he went "because of a revelation," perhaps suggesting that he was not forced to go, and that he did so *privately* rather than *publicly* (Gal 2:2). But intriguingly, Paul does say that one of the things he did in Jerusalem was check to see if he was essentially getting nowhere fast with his ministry among the gentiles. What is fascinating here is that the language he uses to describe his concern parallels Isaiah 49 once more:

Gal 2:2d: . . . lest I was running, or ran, in vain.

Paul.

> **Isa 49:4a LXX:** I said, "I labored in vain, and for emptiness and for nothing I gave my strength ..."

Just as the servant expresses doubts about his calling by talking as if he exerted all of his effort for nothing, Paul too does the same here.

The net effect of these allusions to Isaiah 49 in the autobiography seems to be that Paul is reflecting widely on his calling to the gentiles in the light of the Galatian crisis. Perhaps he hopes Isaiah 49 will bolster his confidence in the face of any self-doubt that may have creeped in.[5] It is worth noting that Acts records that when Paul was in Pisidian Antioch (i.e., south Galatia) during his first missionary journey, he quoted Isaiah 49 to them, saying that the Lord "commanded" them with the following: "I have placed you for a light to the nations, in order for you to be for salvation unto the end of the earth" (Acts 13:47; cf. Isa 49:6 LXX). Undertaking the work of the servant from Isaiah 49 seems to be part of what Paul means by saying that he is not a people pleaser, but a slave of the Messiah (Gal 1:10).

If the first movement of the autobiography stresses that Paul spent so little time with the Jerusalem apostles, the second section (Gal 2:1–10) highlights that Paul had a mutual understanding with them, and the third reveals (Gal 2:11–21) that *they* needed to be corrected by him. Paul may be narrating these stories to correct false reports about what happened, but as we will see, they continue to reinforce that Paul is a slave of the Messiah.

---

5. For more on the significance of Paul's use of Isaiah in Galatians, see Harmon, *She Must and Shall Go Free*.

THE MESSIAH'S SLAVE IN JERUSALEM (GALATIANS 2:1-10)

In the second segment, when Paul went to Jerusalem with Barnabas and Titus, Paul says that the pillar apostles gave him and Barnabas the right hand of fellowship and recognized that he had his own sphere of ministry to the uncircumcised just as Peter had received a ministry to the circumcised (Gal 2:7-9). The pillar apostles also did not change or adjust Paul's gospel in any way (Gal 2:6), except they "added" that he should "remember the poor," which he quickly affirms was something he was eagerly doing already (Gal 2:10). In this way Paul can insist that his authority and gospel were neither derivative in content nor secondary in authority.

Yet when Paul first went down to Jerusalem for this private meeting, there were some "false siblings" who wanted Paul's Greek companion, Titus, to be circumcised (Gal 2:3). The passage in Greek is a bit muddled here because Paul seems to lose his train of thought (perhaps due to frustration while dictating), but despite that fact, the point he is making is very clear: Paul and his companions did not give in to the *compulsion* to circumcise Titus, they did not *surrender* to them, and they did not become their *slaves* (Gal 2:3-5). Giving in to compulsion for Paul, then, is fundamentally *enslaving*. Instead, they clung to their freedom in Christ and "the truth of the gospel," resisting these "false siblings" (Gal 2:5). Again, Paul is a slave of no one except the Messiah (Gal 1:10).

THE MESSIAH'S SLAVE IN ANTIOCH
(GALATIANS 2:11-21)

In the third and final section of the autobiography, Paul narrates a confrontation with Peter in Antioch.[6] Before "people from James" came, Peter was eating with gentiles, but then he began to withdraw, Paul says, because he was afraid of "those from the circumcision." What exactly Peter was doing and why he withdrew is a matter of some debate. Most likely the issue was the fact that he was eating *with gentiles* rather than eating gentile food. Even in Acts 10–11, where Peter receives a vision of unclean animals and is told to eat them, he does not interpret the vision as indicating that he should change his diet or have a BBQ. Peter recognizes that the vision means that he should welcome gentiles like Cornelius. But here in Antioch, by withdrawing, Paul says that Peter's actions had the effect of *compelling* the gentiles to Judaize and that his actions were not in step with "the truth of the gospel" (Gal 2:14). In other words, from Paul's perspective this was tantamount to what happened with Titus in Jerusalem because it's as if Peter would only eat with people who were circumcised. And just as with Titus, Paul resists this effort to compel gentiles to Judaize.

Paul then rattles off a series of arguments explaining why Peter was in the wrong (Gal 2:15–21). The heart of Paul's response to Peter is an appeal to the way that justification works. God as the judge of all declares people to be "in the right" or "innocent" in his courtroom on the same basis regardless of whether they are Jews or gentiles. That common basis is not observance of the law, but faith (Gal 2:15–17).

---

6. This is not the same Antioch as Pisidian Antioch; it is the Antioch just above the Syrian border in modern-day Antakya, Turkey (Türkiye), also known as Antioch-on-the-Orontes.

It is possible, because the original Greek is ambiguous in Gal 2:16, that Paul is saying either that people are justified by *faith in Christ* or by *the faithfulness of Christ*. This is part of what is commonly known as the *pistis Christou* debate. This debate, which I am intentionally simplifying, need not distract us much, but it's worth articulating what difference it does and doesn't make. Technically, in two places in Gal 2:16 the Greek reads "faith of (Jesus) Christ." The question is whether this faith refers to Jesus's own faithfulness, or someone's faith in him. Take a look at the four main lines of Gal 2:16 in the verse below:

1. We know that a person is not justified by works of the law, but through *faith of Jesus Christ*,
2. and we believed in Christ Jesus,
3. in order that we might be justified by *faith of Christ*, and not by works of the law,
4. because by works of the law no flesh will be justified.

The phrases in italics in lines 1 and 3, which I've left ambiguous, can be translated either way. If we went with "the faithfulness of (Jesus) Christ" in each case, that would make it very clear that justification is possible because of what Christ accomplished. Of course, the reason why Paul wants people to believe in Christ is precisely because of what he has done for them. And the only way to receive this gift is to accept it by faith, which line 2 makes clear without any ambiguity. So, although there is great debate here, I don't think it makes a major theological difference; ultimately, it is both. That being said, I do find the translation "faith in (Jesus) Christ" to be more compelling, since the logic seems to work like this: line 1 gives the conditions for justification, line 2 states that those conditions have been met, and line 3 expresses the result of meeting the condition.

But there's more to Paul's point to Peter about why justification works like this. If justification was through law observance, rather than faith (however we understand it), that would mean that God's gift of Christ has been nullified (Gal 2:21). This is because, by being crucified with Christ, believers have died to the law and now live lives animated afresh by his resurrected life (Gal 2:18–20). In Paul's response to Peter, he uses first-person language (i.e., "I have been crucified with Christ" in Gal 2:19), but since he is speaking from their common knowledge as Jews (i.e., "we are Jews by nature" in Gal 2:15) and their shared reality in the Messiah, it is not the case that Paul alone has experienced these things. What Paul has experienced is emblematic of life in the Messiah—for Paul, for Jews, and for gentiles too. Paul is a paradigm of what it looks like to follow the Messiah properly, in Paul's words, as a slave of the Messiah—someone who trusts in him alone and resists the compulsion to become slaves of anyone else.

As we have seen, in addition to clearing up misinformation and setting the record straight with respect to the pillar apostles in Jerusalem, Paul also wants to present himself clearly as a slave of the Messiah in the autobiography. I think we ought to keep both of these intentions in mind when we read these chapters. Elsewhere Paul demonstrates that he wants the Galatians to imitate him when he directly appeals to his time with them, saying "Be like me" (Gal 4:12). He calls the Galatians to be like him in part because of the turmoil and hardship that they are experiencing presently with their social dislocation, communal strife, and fears associated with undergoing circumcision itself. This seems to be why Paul reminds them of his own experience of persecution and closely aligns himself with the cross, even drawing attention to "the marks of Jesus" that he bears (Gal 6:17)—marks which incidentally refer to the branding marks that typically designated someone as a slave. At the beginning of the letter and at the close of it, Paul points to the fact that he is a slave of the Messiah. Just as Paul resisted compulsion to become slaves of others out of a commitment to the Messiah (Gal 2:3, 14), so too the Galatians are to do likewise (Gal 6:12). And just as Paul portrays Christ in his cruciform life,[7] so too he wants Christ to be fully formed in them (Gal 4:19). Paul is a paradigm for Galatian imitation in the present crisis.

REFLECTIONS

1. What seems to be the *primary* purpose of the autobiography to you: for Paul to defend himself against accusations, to present himself to the Galatians in a certain way, or perhaps something else?
2. How does the famous passage about justification by faith take on new significance when we read it as the conclusion of the autobiographical section of the letter and as part of Paul's response to Peter in Antioch?

---

7. On the pattern of Christian living as shaped by the cross, see esp. Gorman, *Cruciformity*.

6

PAUL'S RESPONSE TO THE GALATIANS, PART TWO

The Law Protected the Promise to Abraham

THE SECOND FEATURE OF PAUL'S response to the Galatians concerns the role of the law for Abraham's entire family, inclusive of Jews and gentiles. Paul obviously has a lot to say about the law in Galatians, but scholars understand how Paul treats the topic of the law very differently. Looking back at our reading strategies from chapter 2, traditional approaches to Galatians prior to the mid-twentieth century have tended to read Paul's critical comments about the law as pertaining to part of the law (i.e., ceremonial and civic laws) or to improperly using the law (i.e., legalistically, or to earn salvation). In popular expressions of Protestant readings, the "works of the law" often become inflated beyond the Mosaic law to include any "good works" whatsoever. Proponents of the New Perspective on Paul have highlighted how ancient Jews weren't legalists trying to earn their salvation, nor did they separate out moral laws from other ones. So these interpreters proposed that Paul had the whole Mosaic law in mind, but "works of the law" refer to those specific practices that separate Jews from gentiles, such as circumcision, Sabbath keeping, and dietary restrictions. Since one of the things that is noteworthy about how Paul addresses the law, especially in Galatians 3–4, is that he assigns it a temporary role, apocalyptic interpreters of Paul have often seen an emphasis on the radical newness of what God is doing in the Messiah. The Paul within Judaism crowd, however, believe that Paul remained Torah observant and that he expected Jews to continue to be observant as well. So then, whatever Paul says about the law that seems to be negative, must not be about how the law relates to Jews, but only how it relates to gentiles.

Wading through these options can be tricky, not least because these are reading strategies for understanding Paul as a whole, not just Galatians. But one of the very first things that we need to acknowledge about the law is that it was not meant for gentiles. It was not a universal law for all of humanity, but a very specific covenant that legislates the people of Israel. This is why Paul speaks in terms of "Judaization" when he confronts Peter in Antioch (Gal 2:14); if the gentiles adopt circumcision and begin practicing the law, they are no longer gentiles, but instead they have become Jews. Yet because works of the law had nothing to do with the Galatians receiving the Spirit of God's Son (Gal 3:2, 5), and also had nothing to do with them being justified and declared to be in the right before him (Gal 2:16), the gentiles in Galatia do not need to become Jews in order to come into God's favor or to be adopted into the family. Because of this fact, Peter should not have withdrawn from the tables in Antioch (Gal 2:12), but should have continued to gather around the table with them, just like families do.

Indeed, this is because the law does not legislate the entirety of Abraham's family.

Paul makes a number of crucial points to establish that the law does not legislate the one family of Abraham, with the primary emphasis being that the law had a temporary function in service of God's promise to Abraham. Paul overviews the history of Israel three times in Gal 3:6—4:7 with respect to the law's role until the time when the promises began to be realized. The three historical overviews can be seen in Gal 3:6-14; 3:15-29; and 4:1-7 respectively, which are then followed by the final argument involving Abraham, which is the infamous allegory of Gal 4:21—5:1.

THE FIRST HISTORICAL OVERVIEW IN GALATIANS 3:6-14

The first overview begins with overt attention on Abraham. As Paul explains, God promised Abraham that the nations would be blessed through him (Gal 3:8). This blessing occurs when the nations share in the same faith that Abraham had (Gal 3:9), which is the same faith that put Abraham in right standing before God prior to being circumcised (Gal 3:6; cf. Gen 15:6). Just as we say "like father, like son," the nations also become Abraham's sons, or children, by bearing the family resemblance (Gal 3:7).[1] I prefer to translate the Greek terms *huios/huioi* as "son/s" rather than as "child/ren," here and elsewhere in Galatians, because of the way that sonship is linked to ancient conventions of inheritance. But the beautiful thing is that although the Greek term is masculine, no one is excluded from receiving this inheritance by faith on the basis of gender (cf. Gal 3:28-29). The experience of the gentiles receiving the Spirit by faith is

1. For more on Abrahamic sonship in Paul's argument, see Bekken, *Paul's Negotiation*.

relevant to the story of Abraham (note the "even as" in Gal 3:6), because they were experiencing the realization of the promise that the nations would be blessed through him.

But before this promise could come to the gentiles, Paul highlights that the curse of the law had to be addressed first (Gal 3:10). The curse of the law does not come upon all of humanity, since not all of humanity had the law or knew what it requires, but rather it comes upon those who possessed the law ("as many as are from works of the law"), referring to the people of Israel. Since the law states that a curse comes upon those who do not remain in and do the things prescribed in the law (Gal 3:10; cf. Deut 27:26), Israel came under the law's curse, the chief of which was death, which at the national level was often a way of referring to their exile from the land, as outlined in Deuteronomy 27–32. Once the curse of the law was addressed, namely by Christ becoming a curse on the cross (Gal 3:13), the blessing of Abraham could be in Christ, and the promise of the Spirit could be received through faith (Gal 3:14).

THE SECOND HISTORICAL OVERVIEW IN GALATIANS 3:15–29

The justification by faith that Abraham experienced, and the promise that the nations would be blessed, obviously precede the law's curse, but in the second historical overview, it is even more significant for Paul that the promise precedes the time when the law was given. It matters to Paul that the law did not even come onto the scene for another four hundred and thirty years after God made promises to Abraham (Gal 3:17). Thus, the promises must take priority. He adds that the promises were given to Abraham *and to his seed*, which Paul surprisingly takes to mean, not all of his biological descendants, but specifically one of them—the

Messiah (Gal 3:16). It likewise matters to Paul that unlike the promise, which was given directly to Abraham, the law was mediated through angels and Moses (simply referred to here as "the mediator"). The Johnny-come-lately law, then, must have had a temporary role, Paul concludes, designed to address transgressions in the meantime until the promises arrived (Gal 3:19–25). Paula Fredriksen reminds readers that Paul claims elsewhere that the law came with privileges (cf. Rom 3:1–2; 9:4–5), and that it was holy, righteous, and good (Rom 7:12). For these reasons, according to her, Paul could not have said these things in Galatians with respect to *the Jewish relationship* to the law.[2] But I would say in response that in Galatians we see that the law had a holy, righteous, and good *role to play*. Indeed, even in Romans itself we see language that suggests that the law played a temporary role as well (cf., e.g., Rom 4:13–15; 7:1–5).

The law's purpose for the time before the arrival of the Messiah is exemplified by the specific use of the term "guardian" (Gal 3:24–25), which speaks to its temporary role in keeping something safe until it is no longer necessary to do so. Just like those in the Night's Watch who "take the black" in *Game of Thrones* and who protect the Realm from what lies North of the Wall, after the coming of the Messiah, Paul can say of the law, "and now its watch is ended." The law doesn't go away, of course, but after the arrival of the Messiah its role has changed. But since the term "guardian" on its own does not quite speak to the inherent temporary role of the Greek term underlying this, *paidagōgos*, which is a kind of guardian specifically assigned to children in the ancient world, N. T. Wright has chosen the term "babysitter" in his translation. This does the job decently well for modern readers, but it can come across as slightly humorous, as I know from experience when I gave a full

2. Fredriksen, *Paul*, 86.

reading of Wright's translation of Galatians for the opening reception of the 2013 Scripture and Theology Conference dedicated to Galatians at the University of St Andrews. The entire reading that night was appropriately solemn and reverent until I uttered the words, "we are no longer under the rule of the babysitter."[3] I am not sure what a preferable term would be, but if "the rule of the babysitter" did not elicit such snickering that day, I would think "babysitter" is probably one of our best contemporary English options.

Nevertheless, with the arrival of the promised Messiah, all those who have faith in the Messiah have become sons of God (Gal 3:26). Furthermore, all those baptized into Christ, have put Christ on like a garment, and have become one in Christ (Gal 3:27-28). Thus, by virtue of being part of Christ—the promised offspring of Abraham to whom the promises were given—the Galatians are part of the offspring of Abraham and are themselves now heirs of those same promises made to Abraham and the Messiah (Gal 3:29; cf. 3:16). They did not become part of Abraham's offspring through a Judaizing process that would have included adopting the law and receiving circumcision. Instead, they became part of the family by sharing in the faith of father Abraham, and by becoming one with his offspring, the Messiah, through faith and baptism.

THE THIRD HISTORICAL OVERVIEW IN GALATIANS 4:1-7

The primary points of the second historical overview in Gal 3:15-29, such as the way Paul articulates the temporal role of the law relative to God's promises (Gal 3:15-25) followed by the realization of the promise in faith and baptism (Gal 3:26-29), are essentially repeated again in the

3. See now the 3rd ed.: Wright, *New Testament for Everyone*, 359.

third historical overview in Gal 4:1–7, although with some slightly different imagery. Paul compares Israel's status under the law—during that same temporary period in which the law was like a "guardian" or "babysitter" for Israel—to the way that sons grow up in a Roman household. Roman sons essentially had the same rights as a slave when they were young, being under the authority of others during that time, which Paul calls "stewards" and "managers," even though they were destined to inherit everything "at the date set by the father" (Gal 4:1–2).[4] Once again, we see the same pattern of temporary governance leading to the realization of the promise—the same inheritance that Paul has already mentioned for the offspring of Abraham (Gal 3:29).

If the link to inheritance and the temporary role of these stewards and managers in Gal 4:1–2 did not already make us think that this was a metaphor reiterating what Paul has described in Gal 3:15–29, Paul makes the comparison clear in what follows. He says that the cosmic *stoicheia* (whatever they may be; more on this below) enslaved "us" when "we were young" until "the fullness of time" came when God sent his Son to redeem "those under the law" and to provide "adoption" (Gal 4:3–5).[5] Again, Paul here describes a similar temporal situation that culminates in the arrival of the promised one. It is important to note that although the *stoicheia* here were an enslaving force during the same period in which the law addressed matters of transgressions (Gal 3:19) and functioned to imprison those under it (Gal 3:23), that does not make the law one of the *stoicheia*. The simple reason is because sin itself was also an enslaving force during this time (Gal 3:22), and the law is obviously not sinful! Instead, the law brings knowledge of sin, and reveals where people have transgressed. Just

4. See Goodrich, "Guardians, Not Taskmasters."
5. On the adoption metaphor here, see Heim, *Adoption*.

as other powers were operative, taking advantage of these conditions, so also the cosmic *stoicheia* were an enslaving force as well. Paul similarly describes in Rom 7:7–25 how sin and death tried to co-opt the law and leverage it for their purposes (whether these are personifications or not), and so we should not conflate the law with either sin or the *stoicheia* in Galatians.

Scholars are divided on what exactly these *stoicheia* are (e.g., "elementary principles," "the four elements of the world," "astral spirits," etc.), but I tend to think they are spiritual beings associated with the stars. The main reason that I think this is because Paul refers to them again as "not gods by nature" (Gal 4:8–9) before he describes what turning back to serving these *stoicheia* looks like in terms of keeping the calendar: "you are keeping days, months, seasons, and years" (Gal 4:10).[6] Three of those four calendrical terms appear in Gen 1:14 LXX to refer to the governance of the stars over the calendar, making astral spirits the most likely interpretation of the *stoicheia*, in my opinion. For our purposes we only need to acknowledge that the *stoicheia* are here an enslaving force operative during the time that the law functioned as a "guardian" over Israel, but the law is not one of the *stoicheia*.

Just like how the first and second historical overviews in Galatians 3 conclude with the initial realization of the promises made to Abraham, so too the third one in Galatians 4 ends with the reception of the Spirit after the "fullness of time" when Christ arrived. The Spirit is given to those who are *already sons* (Gal 4:6; cf. "because you are sons"), since they are sons of God by faith (Gal 3:26).[7] Just as doing the law had nothing to do with the Galatians

6. Cf. Arnold, "Returning to the Domain of the Powers."

7. Contrary to the thesis of Hodge, *If Sons*. See Hewitt, "Πνεῦμα." Cf. Song, *One Spirit*, 170–87.

receiving the Spirit (Gal 3:2, 5), so too it had nothing to do with them becoming part of the family of Abraham and indeed the family of God. Both sonship and the Spirit are conferred by faith. The Spirit confirms this status of sonship, being the Spirit of God's own Son no less (Gal 4:6). And this confirmation is heard in the so-called "Abba cry"; the sons who receive the Spirit cry out to God, "Abba, Father." (The word Greek "Father" [*pater*] provides the immediate interpretation of the Aramaic *Abba*, so despite what you have likely heard, Abba does not mean "Daddy.")[8] The Spirit confirms sonship, even in the instances that prompt people to cry out to him most for assurance of his love and care, such as when all signs around them seem to suggest the opposite. This is just like what we see when Jesus cried out "Abba, Father" in Gethsemane in the midst of his pain and uncertainty (Mark 14:36), and also just like how Paul writes about how the "Abba cry" confirms a believers' status as a child of God, and hence an heir, provided they also suffer with Christ (Rom 8:15–17). Even in times of intense hardship, the Spirit of the Son provides confirmation that God is their Father.

Although the Spirit is given to the sons who stand to receive an inheritance, the Spirit is not the full inheritance itself. The one who receives the Spirit is an heir, just like the Messiah is an heir as Abraham's offspring (Gal 3:29). The full inheritance itself is most likely the kingdom of God, since that is the object of the verb "inherit" in Gal 5:21, where it says that those producing the works of the flesh will not inherit the kingdom. That connection also makes the most sense of the metaphors in Gal 4:1–7, since a Roman son, who is no greater than a slave while he is young, is destined to be "lord of all" (Gal 4:2), which hints at the regal future that awaits him. This is part of the glorious future

---

8. Barr, "'Abbā Isn't 'Daddy.'"

that the Galatians themselves participate in. As Paul says to conclude this paragraph:

> **Gal 4:7:** So you are no longer a slave but a son, and if a son, then an heir through God.

The possession of the Spirit confirms this, which is why Paul could so confidently say that the only thing he wants to learn from them is how they first received the Spirit (Gal 3:2). The answer to that question confirms so many things about who the Galatians are that to receive circumcision at best ignores this fact, and at worst rejects it (cf. Gal 4:11).

THE ALLEGORICAL ARGUMENT IN GALATIANS 4:21—5:1

After Paul's personal appeal in Gal 4:12-20, he offers one more argument about how the gentiles are part of Abraham's family already, and they did not need to be circumcised to be part of it. This is part of the infamous allegorical argument that Paul makes about Abraham's two sons. The passage is convoluted and hard to follow, so we won't go deep into all of the details. I remember when I first sat down with N. T. Wright in St Andrews for a supervision at the start of my doctoral studies. Towards the end of our time I was suddenly curious and had to ask him what the one question is that he never wants to be asked when he has an open time of "Q&A" after a speaking engagement. His response was quick and animated—"the meaning of the allegory of Galatians 4!" And so, it is with fear and trepidation that we proceed.

In the allegory, the gentiles' sonship to Abraham is compared to Isaac, who was "born according to promise" (Gal 4:28). Just as Isaac's birth was brought about by a radical promise of God to Abraham and Sarah in their old age

(Gal 4:23), an act that essentially brought life out of death (cf. Rom 4:17, 19), so too the gentiles owe their sonship to Abraham by means that go beyond the flesh and lineal descent (Gal 4:31). Those born of the "free woman," referring to Sarah, are thus likewise free, and the "Jerusalem above" is their mother (Gal 4:26), whereas those born of the "slave woman," referring to Abraham's handmaid, Hagar, are likewise enslaved. Ishmael is thus also a child of Abraham, but Paul interprets his birth through Hagar the handmaid as coming about through the flesh rather than through the work of God.

It seems to me that Paul arrived at such a reading of Genesis, not by Genesis itself, but through reading Isaiah. In chapter 5 we saw that Paul was reflecting widely on Isaiah 49 to assure him of his calling to the nations, and here in the allegory he cites Isa 54:1 LXX in Gal 4:27, which reads:

> **Gal 4:27:** For it is written,
> "Rejoice, O barren one who does not give birth,
> Come forth and cry out, O you without birth
>   pains,
> Because many are the children of the desolate
>   one,
> More than the one who has a husband."

The language of barrenness and a large offspring is reminiscent of Sarah and the Abrahamic promise. In fact, Sarah is famously only mentioned in Isa 51:1–2 outside of Genesis in the entire OT.[9] Thus, it seems that Isaiah is really the horse pulling the cart for Paul's reading of Genesis, and the references to two women in Isa 54:1, which compare Jerusalem before and after the exile, are read back onto Abraham's relationships with Sarah and Hagar.[10]

9. Hays, *Echoes of Scripture*, 120.
10. For more on this, see Dunne, *Persecution and Participation*, 179–91.

The reality of Isaiah 54 is accomplished because of the suffering of the servant in Isaiah 53, and so it is unsurprising that Paul also highlights elements of suffering in his allegory of Genesis in what follows. The gentile Christ-followers are now compared to Isaac because of how they are being treated by those associated with the flesh (cf. Gen 21:9):

> **Gal 4:29:** But just as then the one born according to the flesh persecuted the one born according to the Spirit, so also it is now.

Suffering is another feature of family resemblance that shows that the Galatians belong to the family of Abraham. Suffering does not undermine their sonship, nor is it antithetical to their life in the Spirit (Gal 3:4; 4:6). This likewise means that the agitators bear the family resemblance too, but their persecuting activity reveals that they belong to Ishmael's side of the family.[11] By making these connections between the present crisis and the two sons of Abraham, it is as if Paul has reached that point in a pick-up game of basketball where it is no longer clear to everyone who's on whose team, and so the teams split up into "shirts" and "skins"—and obviously those promoting gentile circumcision are on team "skins"! Paul is thus teasing out that being a son of Abraham is not actually sufficient, because if you're not a child of Abraham like Isaac, then you do not stand to inherit.

> **Gal 4:30:** But what does the Scripture say? "Cast out the slave woman and her son; for the son of

---

11. Heinsch (*Figure of Hagar*) argues instead that, based on Second Temple Jewish understandings of Hagar as a non-Jew, Paul is talking about the former lives of his gentile readers here before "the free woman" and "the Jerusalem above" became their mother in Christ. For reasons that I articulate in this section, I understand this passage to relate to the Galatian crisis differently.

the slave woman will not inherit with the son of the free woman."

These words, adapted from Gen 21:10 LXX, were spoken by Sarah about Hagar, and Paul undoubtedly uses Sarah's words to warn the agitators about their ultimate fate,[12] but he also seems to be using her words to command the Galatians to disfellowship from the agitators and thus to expel them from their communities.[13] This is not a surprising move when we remember what Paul says elsewhere in the letter. To start, Paul pronounces a curse upon them for deviating from his gospel (Gal 1:8–9).[14] For Paul it does not matter who diverges from that message. Even an angel who strays will come under Paul's curse. And as we saw in chapter 4, these troublemakers were no angels. Because of that, he also says that they will bear the judgment (Gal 5:10) in an allusion to the final judgment. In the meantime, he wishes that they be castrated for the turmoil that they have caused (Gal 5:12). He also potentially alludes to expulsion by comparing their influence to leavened dough (Gal 5:9), which is reminiscent of how he uses the same metaphor elsewhere for that very purpose (cf. 1 Cor 5:6–13). Their expulsion speaks to the fact that they, being fleshly and aggressive like Ishmael, will not inherit alongside the promised children born according to the Spirit (Gal 4:30), just as those doing the divisive works of the flesh will not inherit the kingdom of God relative to those who produce the fruit of the Spirit (Gal 5:19–23).

By succumbing in the midst of the persecution surrounding circumcision, the Galatians themselves could also

12. Eastman, "'Cast Out The Slave Woman.'"

13. For a defense of this, see Dunne, "Cast Out The Aggressive Agitators."

14. For more on the significance of Paul pronouncing a curse to mitigate deviation, see Kim, *Curse Motifs*.

compromise the inheritance that will come to the children of the free woman (Gal 4:30). This is what is implied earlier when Paul began this argument by asking, in the context of discussing their initial and ongoing reception of the Spirit, "Did you suffer so much in vain?" (Gal 3:4). To give in to the pressure to be circumcised (i.e., to be "perfected by the flesh," cf. Gal 3:3) is to render their suffering all for naught, jeopardizing the inheritance that comes to those in possession of the Spirit.

Paul concludes the allegory by calling the Galatians to "stand firm" in the midst of persecution and "not submit again to a yoke of slavery" (Gal 5:1). To receive circumcision in this context would be like trying to become a son of Abraham through Hagar, through the flesh. That road leads to slavery, Paul says. But just as Paul resisted compulsion to slavery with respect to gentile circumcision and Judaization (Gal 2:3, 14), he calls them to do the same. The law is not what made the Galatians sons, and so it does not govern their ongoing lives as sons either. This is because, as sons, they have the divine Spirit, which means that they now exist in a sphere beyond the law's legislation.

REFLECTIONS

1. What role do you think the Mosaic law continues to have after the arrival of the Messiah now that its role as a "guardian" has ended?

2. Do you think Paul's allegorical reading of Genesis is warranted? Can Christians today approach Scripture in the same way?

7

PAUL'S RESPONSE TO THE GALATIANS, PART THREE

Those with the Spirit Are Above the Law

THE THIRD FEATURE OF PAUL'S response to the Galatians that is crucial to recognize when reading Galatians is how Paul talks about new life in the Spirit.[1] This is the direct corollary to Paul's argument that the law had a temporary role as a "guardian." Paul stresses that those who possess the Spirit are, if you like, outside the law's jurisdiction. This argument begins initially with the observation that the Spirit did not come to them by means of the law (Gal 3:2, 5), but it is further developed when Paul intimates that the law does not possess the ability to make things alive—the purview of the Spirit.[2]

---

1. On the role of the Spirit in Galatians, see, e.g., J. Williams, *Spirit, Ethics, and Eternal Life*; Buchanan, *Spirit, New Creation, and Christian Identity*.

2. On this broader theme in Galatians, and how life and the Spirit

LAW & LIFE

Paul makes it very clear that the law is unable to produce life when he says, "if a law was given that was able to make alive, righteousness would be from the law" (Gal 3:21b). The law can only bring knowledge of what it prescribes, but it cannot make someone keep it, nor can it empower law-fulfillment. It has no ability to animate people at all, and it cannot bring the dead back to life either. The Spirit can do all of that, however. Earlier in the letter Paul gives a few glimpses of how the law is not associated with life.

The first glimpse of this theme before Gal 3:21 is when Paul says, "through the law, I died to the law, in order that I might live to God" (Gal 2:19a–b). This is a startling claim in many respects, not least because one would assume that the law made it possible to "live to God." But this point hints at the theme of the law's inability to lead to life that Paul is developing. (I will circle back to what the significance of dying to the law might be momentarily.)

The second glimpse prior to Gal 3:21 occurs within the argument of 3:10–14. Paul writes:

> **Gal 3:11–12:** It is evident that no one is justified by the law before God, because "the righteous will live by faith." Now, the law is not from faith, but "the one doing them will live by them."

Paul seems to be juxtaposing two biblical passages that refer to life and living, one from Habakkuk and one from Leviticus. And he seems to be implying that *eschatological life* is offered to those who do the law (Lev 18:5 LXX) or, alternatively it seems, to those who have faith (Hab 2:4 LXX). Jason Staples has recently argued that we should view Paul as reading both passages messianically to speak of how

---

relate to justification, see Boakye, *Death and Life*.

Jesus's resurrection was tied to his obedience and fidelity.[3] I tend to read the paragraph as speaking more broadly than the Messiah here (i.e., "*no one* is justified by the law before God"), but I don't think there is such a strong antithesis between the two passages, as Staples rightly points out.[4] The problem with Lev 18:5's promise of life for those who do the law is not that it is an alternative option, but rather that the curse of the law (Gal 3:10–11) keeps this promise from being realized. The law can promise life, but it cannot *make someone alive* (Gal 3:21). Yet Christ addressed the law's curse (Gal 3:13), so that the Spirit could be poured out (Gal 3:14), and so that empowered living beyond the law's curse could occur (cf. Rom 8:3–4).

The way that the Spirit is associated with life in the letter is seen not least through the fertile image of the ninefold fruit of the Spirit (Gal 5:22–23), but also the language of sowing to the Spirit and reaping eternal life (Gal 6:7–9). The work of the Spirit is most likely implied when Paul refers to "new creation" in Gal 6:15, even though Gal 6:11–17 does not explicitly mention the Spirit. Each of these passages also addresses, by implication at least, the Spirit's ability to enliven with respect to matters of law observance. Taking these in reverse order, we see that the "new creation" is what ultimately matters relative to the binary of circumcision and foreskin (Gal 6:15). Sowing to the Spirit is contrasted to sowing to one's own flesh, which leads to corruption, and in this letter, sowing to the flesh must speak to the matter of receiving circumcision (Gal 6:8).

With the fruit of the Spirit, Paul also directly comments on how the law relates to it:

---

3. Staples, *Paul and the Resurrection of Israel*, 221–70.
4. Staples, *Paul and the Resurrection of Israel*, 255–64.

> **Gal 5:22-23:** Now the fruit of the Spirit is love, joy, peace, patience, kindness, goodness, faith, gentleness, self-control. There is no law dealing with such people.

Most translations say something like "against such things there is no law," but I am persuaded by Logan Williams that the term often rendered "things" best relates to the people who manifest the Spirit's fruit in their lives rather than the fruit themselves.[5] This creates a nice parallel with the vice list about the flesh since that portion concludes with a comment about people: "those doing such things will not inherit the kingdom of God." In this way both the vice list and the virtue list end with a comment on people. But what does it mean that "there is no law dealing with such people"? In some sense this must mean that the work of the Spirit makes people beyond the law's ability to legislate. The law does not deal with people who have the divine *pneuma* or Spirit (i.e., "pneumatic beings").[6]

LAW & DEATH

The reason why the law is not binding for pneumatic beings is because the law is only operative and binding until death. Paul articulates this with respect to marriage in Rom 7:1–5. As he says "the law rules over a person as long as he lives" (Rom 7:1b), and so a woman is released from the law of marriage when her husband dies (Rom 7:2–3). This analogy is then applied to the Mosaic law: "So, my siblings,

5. See L. Williams, "Being(s) Above the Law." As he points out, there is also a parallel expression that gives warrant to this rendering of the preposition *kata* in Aristotle, *Politics* 3:8 1284a.

6. As with other scholars more recently, I prefer the term "pneumatic beings" over "spiritual ones," because the term "spiritual" is so vacuous in today's culture and misses the transformative nature of the animating presence of the Spirit.

you also died to the law through the body of the Messiah for you to be joined to another, who was raised from the dead, in order that you might bear fruit to God" (Rom 7:4). The comment at the end about bearing fruit provides a nice point of comparison with the preceding discussion on the fruit of the Spirit, but moreover, the point in Romans 7 about the law governing up until the time of death is also applicable in Galatians.

Remember how Paul said, "through the law, I died to the law" (Gal 2:19)? Paul was ascribing that reality to his participation in the death and crucifixion of Christ (Gal 2:19-20). This seems to be why Paul says that he cannot rebuild what he tore down in the previous verse: "for if I rebuild again what I tore down, I show myself to be a transgressor" (Gal 2:18). The "tearing down" occurred in his death to the law, as he goes on to describe in verses 19-20:

> **Gal 2:19-20:** For through the law, I died to the law, in order that I might live to God. I have been crucified with Christ. No longer do I live, but the Messiah lives in me. And the life I now live in the flesh, I live by faith in the Son of God, who loved me and gave himself for me.

This is not just an experience that Paul had, as we saw in chapter 5. Indeed, Paul even says that "those who belong to Christ have crucified the flesh with its passions and desires" (Gal 5:24). Furthermore, Paul was speaking these words at the end of Galatians 2 to Peter in Antioch, "we are Jews by nature" (Gal 2:15), and so this reality is not just for gentiles. The Paul within Judaism perspective tends to view Paul's pneumatology as solving the gentile problem, but it also solves the Jewish plight, since all are under sin and subject to death (cf. Rom 3:9-18, 23). Paul's speech to Peter highlights the Jewish need for the gift of new life in the Messiah (Gal 2:15-21). Similarly, in Gal 3:10-14, if the curse of the law was removed so that "we might receive the promise of the Spirit" (Gal 3:14), this would certainly include Jewish believers, if it did not exclusively refer to them, since the curse in this passage is the curse of the Jewish law. Paul's pneumatology is thus for all believers in the Messiah, Jews and gentiles.

So, when do believers participate in this death and experience new life? As Paul says in Romans 6, it is in baptism. And in the great baptismal passage in Galatians 3:26–29, Paul speaks of believers as being so interconnected with Christ through baptism that we can see how the ritual of baptism provides the logic for what Paul says about believers being crucified with Christ. This baptismal reality is also, once again, not just true for gentiles, but also Jews: "there is no Jew nor Greek" (Gal 3:28). All those who have the Spirit of the Messiah, the one who died and yet lives, exist now in a sphere outside of the law's jurisdiction.

LAW & ORDER

Paul speaks fairly straightforwardly about no longer being under the law's authority as a result of life in the Spirit:

> **Gal 5:18:** If you are led by the Spirit, you are not under the law.

Some have thought that "under the law" is shorthand for being under the curse of the law,[7] but that would not work at all for Gal 4:21, when Paul addresses those in Galatia "who want to be under the law." Being "under the law," then, is not about the law's curse, I contend, but the law's authority. To no longer be under it, is to be *above* it. Indeed, life in the Spirit puts one beyond the law's reach.

---

7. T. Wilson, *The Curse of the Law*.

But it is important to say that Paul's logic here is neither antinomian, lawless, nor disorderly. This is also because the Spirit works in the lives of believers to lead them into fulfilling the law, and so they are outside of the law's ability to condemn or curse. As the ninefold fruit of the Spirit demonstrates, the Spirit produces love at the top of the list—the same love that Paul says fulfills the whole law of Moses:[8]

> **Gal 5:13–14:** For you were called in freedom, siblings, only do not use this freedom as an opportunity for the flesh, but through love serve one another. For the whole law is fulfilled in one word, in this: you shall love your neighbor as yourself.

The Spirit also produces faith, the seventh on the list, which justifies us before God (Gal 2:16), and by which we "await the hope of righteousness" (Gal 5:5). If the Spirit's fruit is evident in someone's life they are not going to lie, cheat, murder, steal, etc., and thus the law is not transgressed. But moreover, they will love those around them, and so the law is fulfilled simply by following the Spirit as the Spirit continues to animate their lives. As Paul says, "if we live by the Spirit, let us also walk by the Spirit" (Gal 5:25).

---

8. Once when I was reading a late antique commentary on Galatians by Ambrosiaster (i.e., "false Ambrose"), I was struck by the way that the author pointed out that the *tenfold* fruit of the Spirit was designed to parallel the ten commandments. I could not believe that I had missed something so obvious, and then I realized that this actually meant that the text of Galatians that the author was using had a variant. This variant was in fact a tenth item in the fruit of the Spirit—purity (*hagneia*). The variant is clearly a later secondary addition to the textual tradition, and the desirability of the symbolism of the number ten helps to explain how it got there.

Yet, although the Spirit can be said to function like "moral steroids,"[9] that does not mean that everyone will be "batting a thousand," so to speak. As long as those with the Spirit continue to have the flesh, there will be struggle. But the draw of the flesh is not curtailed by law observance. Rather, it is curtailed by continuing to follow the Spirit. As Paul says:

> **Gal 5:16–17:** Now I say, walk by the Spirit and you will in no way perfect the flesh's desire. For the flesh desires against the Spirit, and the Spirit against the flesh, for these things are opposed to one another, in order that you do the things you don't want to do.

Not "perfecting the flesh's desire" applies to many things, but in the context of the letter it includes the matter of gentile circumcision. The language here mirrors Paul's question about being perfected by the flesh (Gal 3:3), and how backwards that is in the light of the fact that the Galatians have the Spirit. Furthermore, it is even more backwards because the Galatians have "crucified the flesh with its passions and desires" (Gal 5:24). To receive circumcision is to put gentiles back in the fleshly position of slavery they experienced previously before they came to Christ (Gal 4:8–9, 31; 5:1; cf. 2:5), and indeed it cuts them off from spiritual union with Christ (Gal 5:4).[10] In a word, apostasy.

That the flesh will continue to be an issue, is also implied in Gal 2:20. Although Paul has been crucified with Christ (Gal 2:19b), and Christ now lives in him, there's still a life in the flesh that he continues to live (Gal 2:20, "the life I now live in the flesh"). This tension will persist until the

---

9. Cf. Thiessen, *Jewish Paul*, 128, 131.

10. See Ryan Collman's (*Apostle to the Foreskin*, 81–92) intriguing discussion on the consequences of gentile circumcision in Gal 5:2–4.

judgment day at the end of time, which Paul refers to as the harvest. Those who sow to the Spirit will reap eternal life (Gal 6:7–9). What will not lead to life, though, is sowing to the flesh, which, again, must include the procedure of circumcision here, not least because the Greek technically says "the one sowing to his own flesh" (Gal 6:8), making that connection more obvious. The contrast reminds us that what Paul is really getting at is a whole different way of being human in the light of the Spirit's animating presence. And once more, it is not the Mosaic law that guides these people, but that fact does not mean that pneumatic beings are left without a law altogether to guide them until the judgment day.

LAW & JUDGMENT

The law for those who have the Spirit of the Messiah is the Messiah's law. As Paul says:

> **Gal 6:2:** Bear one another's burdens and in this way you will fulfill the Messiah's law.

The Messiah's law may more or less be the Mosaic law taken up into the hands of the Messiah, not least because it is fulfilled through the same kinds of loving acts of service as Paul mentions in 5:13–14. But the Messiah's law, as Galatians makes abundantly clear, would not include several things prescribed in the Mosaic law that do not apply to those gentiles with the Spirit, such as circumcision. Transgressing the Messiah's law must then amount to either, by omission, a failure to display the Spirit's fruit or failing to live out a posture of cruciform love as the Messiah did, or by commission, displaying the works of the flesh in the ongoing struggle of trying to walk by the Spirit (Gal 5:16–17, 26). If such a transgression occurs, those with the Spirit, whom Paul explicitly calls "pneumatic beings" (*pneumatikoi*, i.e., "the Spirit-ual ones"), are supposed to use their Spirit-conferred authority to restore that person who has transgressed (Gal 6:1). They are to do so "by the Spirit who produces gentleness." This is often rendered in English as "by a spirit of gentleness," as if the point of the passage is strictly about the disposition that the Spiritual Ones ought to take. But there are a few reasons why the standard translation is missing something important. First, these people are overtly called "pneumatic beings." The reason why they are called that is because they walk by the Spirit, have their lives animated by the Spirit, and they display the Spirit's fruit, as Paul just discussed in context (Gal 5:18, 22-25). Thus, we should recognize that what they are doing to restore someone who has transgressed is by means of the Spirit's power. And second, gentleness is part of the ninefold fruit of the Spirit. Gentleness comes from the Spirit's influence, and so pneumatic beings rely on the Spirit who produces the fruit of gentleness by which they are able to restore the transgressors in their community.

Paul directly connects reliance on the Spirit with eschatological salvation, saying that in the Spirit "we await the hope of righteousness" (Gal 5:5) and that by sowing to the Spirit we will "reap eternal life" (Gal 6:8-9). These are allusions to the final judgment, the latter example of which Paul alludes to after talking about how pneumatic beings should restore transgressors (Gal 6:1) and bear the burdens of others (Gal 6:2). People are also directly accountable for what they do in the Spirit in relation to the Messiah's law, which Paul addresses with reference to bearing one's "own load" (Gal 6:5). Bearing each other's loads is something we do as we struggle in this life (Gal 6:2), but when it is over, we will all bear our own loads before the judge of the universe.

> **Gal 6:3-5:** For if someone thinks they are something when they are not, they deceive themselves. Let each one test their own work, and then they will be able to boast in themselves alone and not in another person. For each one will bear their own load.

The future judgment setting of bearing loads is clear from other Jewish texts that speak in this way (cf. 4 Ezra 7:104-105), but also from the language of having a "boast" in the future. This refers to what someone will have to show for themselves on that final day.

This point, then, about boasting becomes a rhetorical jab against Paul's opponents in the conclusion of the letter body, because Paul says that whereas his opponents want to boast in the flesh of the Galatians once they receive circumcision (Gal 6:13), Paul only wants to boast in the cross. As he writes:

> **Gal 6:14:** May it never be for me to boast except in the cross of our Lord Jesus Christ, through whom the world was crucified to me, and I to the world.

On the final day, what Paul will boast about is his allegiance to the cross. This is partly why Paul ends the letter by drawing attention to the scars that he received as he revealed the Son to the nations (Gal 1:15-16). As he says:

> **Gal 6:17:** For the time that remains, let no one trouble me. For I bear the marks of Jesus in my body.

He *bears* these marks, and *boasts* in the cross, because on judgment day they are the things that he will cling to, not to anything else. This is partly polemical, though, because Paul also claims that his opponents promote gentile circumcision *to avoid persecution for the cross*. In contrast,

Paul closely identifies himself with the crucified Messiah instead of circumcision. Paul no longer "preaches circumcision" (Gal 5:11), referring to his former insistence on it prior to his transformative encounter with the Messiah. The fact that he does not "preach circumcision" any more is made abundantly clear by his experiences of persecution.[11] Not only do the agitators avoid persecution, but their promotion of gentile circumcision is characterized by Paul *as persecution*. Their display of fleshly division is thus what Paul most likely means then when he says that they do not "keep the law."[12] They do not display the love that fulfills the law of Moses, nor do they bear the Galatians' burdens to fulfill the law of the Messiah. They do not reflect the fruit of the Spirit in their lives, but instead act out the works of the flesh.

LAW & COMMUNITY

When Paul speaks of being crucified to the world, this also further highlights the death and new life pattern of baptism into Christ and new life in the Spirit noted earlier. Again, although the Spirit is not mentioned overtly, the crucifixion of the world in Gal 6:14 gives way to a "new creation" in 6:15, which I take to be the climatic expression of this pattern in the letter. As Paul writes:

> **Gal 6:15:** For neither circumcision is anything, nor foreskin, but a new creation.

---

11. Campbell ("Galatians 5:11") contends that Paul did "preach circumcision" after his transformation, but eventually switched gears to a circumcision-free gospel for gentiles. Yet this seems unlikely in the light of Paul's insistence in Galatians 1–2 that he received his gospel/apostleship directly from Christ.

12. See Dunne, "'They Do Not Keep The Law' (Galatians 6:13)."

In the world that was crucified—what Paul calls "the present evil age" that Jesus provides deliverance from (Gal 1:4)—the binary between circumcision and foreskin held a different significance. But believers have died to that world and thus live in the reality of "new creation" where that binary no longer plays the same role. Scholars debate whether this "new creation" refers to new individuals, a new community, or a new cosmos, or some combination of the three. I think in some sense all three are true, especially when we triangulate other Pauline texts (cf. 2 Cor 5:17; Rom 8:18–25), but here I take *the new community* to be the main focus, not least because "circumcision" and "foreskin" are metonymous for groups of people in Galatians, as when Paul mentions how Peter had a ministry to the circumcision and Paul to the foreskin (Gal 2:7–9). But I also think in terms of a new community because Paul refers to the same binary earlier in Galatians, and speaks of a reality that would be beneficial to the community:

> **Gal 5:6:** For in Christ Jesus neither is circumcision anything, nor foreskin, but faith working itself out through love.

"Faith working itself out through love," means that true faith expresses itself in acts of love. The kind of faith that matters, then, is the kind of faith that when you see it out in the wild, you'd mistake it for love. This is a work of the Spirit, not least because the Spirit produces love and faith as part of the ninefold fruit, but also because the parallel with Gal 6:15 suggests that "faith working itself out through love" is a new creational reality that bolsters the community. The agitators, as we have seen, fail to live by this pattern. As Paul says, they ought to do good to everyone, but especially to fellow believers:

> **Gal 6:10:** Then, as we have time, let us work out what is good with all people, especially with the household of faith.

Although Paul does not mention the agitators here, this comment is a further indictment of their behavior.

Those who live out this new creational identity of faith working through love in the promotion of the community by means of the Spirit's work are called "the Israel of God." As Paul says:

> **Gal 6:16:** As many as will walk by this rule, peace upon them and mercy, even upon the Israel of God.

Walking by "this rule" is the rule of new creation in which the significance of the binary of circumcision and foreskin is properly relegated to the world that was crucified. Paul calls this group the Israel of God because this group of Spirit-led Jews and gentiles do not together comprise a fleshly Israel based on biological descent (cf. "Israel according to the flesh" in 1 Cor 10:18), but rather they are Abraham's offspring (Gal 3:29) just like his child Isaac by an act of God (Gal 4:28, 31). Some people insist instead that this reading cannot be right because "Israel is always Israel," meaning that Paul here refers to ethnic Israel exclusively. But the appellation "Israel *of God*" qualifies the sense in which this group is called "Israel."[13] Other scholars argue

---

13. Furthermore, Staples's recent work on the meaning of the term "Israel" as a broad category inclusive of Jews and non-Jews (i.e., Israelites from the Northern Kingdom who weren't Judean) lends further support to this reading (Staples, *Idea of Israel*). Staples's book on Paul, which builds upon this, shows how the logic of using the term "Israel" to include the nations relates to Paul's expectation of the end-time restoration of the tribes of Israel that were lost through the exile and were merged with the nations, and so Israel's salvation must necessarily include the nations (Staples, *Paul and the Resurrection*

that the grammar should be taken to mean that "peace" is meant for those who walk according to the rule of new creation, but then "mercy" is intended for the Israel of God, as a distinct group. This latter group, according to this view, refers to ethnic Israel who has not recognized her Messiah, and thus Paul wants them to receive "mercy."[14] But divine mercy is not strictly meant for those outside of God's favor or to those threatened with being outside of it (cf., e.g., Matt 5:7; Luke 1:50, 72; Phil 2:27; 1 Tim 1:2). Furthermore, if "Israel of God" does not include Paul's gentile readers in Galatia, then he has completely undermined his entire argument. The Israel of God is the Israel whose mother is the Jerusalem above (Gal 4:26–27). It is the same group qualified by "of God" as the church earlier in Gal 1:13. And, in connection to the theme of those led by the Spirit being beyond the Mosaic law's curse in the present evil age, this Israel observes the Messiah's law and follows the rule of new creation.

CONCLUSION ON PAUL'S RESPONSE TO THE GALATIANS

With this final thread of Paul's response regarding new life in the Spirit, and in keeping with the other two threads from chapters 5 and 6 of this book regarding Paul as a paradigm and the role of the law in protecting the promise to Abraham, we see how Paul is calling the Galatians to avoid circumcision. The law does not legislate the entire family of Abraham, nor does it govern those who possess the Spirit. This does not mean that Jews cannot continue to observe the law, but that is not what Paul addresses in the letter

---

of Israel). For another case of Paul's belief that Gentile inclusion is rooted in Israel's experience of exile, see Starling, *Not My People*.

14. Eastman, "Israel and the Mercy of God."

since he is focused on gentiles. The Paul within Judaism movement sees Paul's silence on Jewish law observance as meaning that Paul presupposes complete observance. I take Paul's silence to allow for its possibility (cf. 1 Cor 7:17–24; 9:19–23), but only when it does not conflict with full gentile inclusion in the Messiah (cf., e.g., Gal 2:10–14). Over and against the Paul within Judaism reading, then, the apocalyptic interpreters of Galatians are right to highlight the elements of newness and discontinuity in Galatians, which are surely there, but this need not be overstated to such a degree, as it often is, that Paul is read as either speaking ill of the law or ignoring Israel's covenantal history. The New Perspective on Paul, which stresses continuity a bit more than the apocalyptic view does, rightly highlights the communal aspects of Jew and gentile relationships in Paul's response to Galatians. But the issue of Jewish ethnocentrism as a target of Paul's concern does not seem to be present, not least because of the socio-cultural factors that likely gave rise to the crisis in Galatia, as the Counter-Imperial reading highlights, even if it sometimes overstates the degree to which Paul tried to address Roman customs and ideology specifically. The Lutheran reading's emphasis on justification by faith as curtailing any notion of human striving before God is surely correct theologically, but this reading's tendency to promote a "Law and Gospel contrast" often lacks the ability to integrate how Paul speaks of the importance of empowered living in the letter, something that Patristic and Medieval interpreters were more clued in on, even if based on a misguided bifurcation of the law into moral and ceremonial elements.

With the three threads of Paul's response to the Galatians, Paul calls for the Galatians to resist the compulsion to be circumcised and not to give in to the pressure they were experiencing from the agitators, just as he himself resisted the compulsion for gentiles to Judaize. The agitators want the circumcision of the flesh, but Paul stresses how incongruous that is with the crucifixion of the flesh. The question that remains for us to address now is whether Paul's response to the crisis in Galatia was effective. Did the Galatians listen to Paul, did they listen to the agitators, or did they just give up?

REFLECTIONS

1. How would you describe the relationship between the Mosaic law and the Messiah's law?

2. How should we think about our own personal agency in the light of the Spirit's work in our lives?

8

WHAT DID THE GALATIANS DO WITH PAUL'S LETTER?

SOMETIME AFTER PAUL WROTE his letter, which was either intended to be a circular letter or was perhaps distributed in multiple copies to the various churches (Gal 1:2),[1] the Galatians would have received it, read it within their communities, and processed it. Perhaps the letter brought welcome news to many (cf. Acts 15:31), but perhaps not, since circumcision, although painful and susceptible to complication (cf. Josephus, *Apion* 2.143), would have relieved their social tension. Perhaps it further exacerbated those tensions, as some may have wanted to remove the agitators from their midst, but others "who want to be under the law" (Gal 4:21) may not have. It may even be that Paul anticipates the pushback when he writes in Gal 6:6, "Let the one teaching the word share in every good thing with the one being taught." By commanding fellowship between teacher

---

1. Meeks, *First Urban Christians*, 143.

and those taught, Paul seems to be intent on ensuring the appropriate care and recognition of those he has appointed to teach the congregations, which may also include anyone he has tasked with explaining the letter as it circulated. But what happened? What did they do with Paul's letter? And what did Paul think they would do?

HOW MUCH CONFIDENCE DID PAUL HAVE IN THE GALATIANS?

We see Paul struggle in real time, it seems, with the prospect of not knowing how things will turn out. Paul expressly states his fears that he may have "labored in vain" over them (Gal 4:11). He conveys his concerns that Christ has not been fully formed within them (Gal 4:19), and he wishes he could be with them in order to, as he says, "change my tone, because I am perplexed by you" (Gal 4:20). But at the same time, Paul does refer to them as "siblings" or "brothers and sisters" (*adelphoi*) at various points in the letter (Gal 1:2, 11; 3:15; 4:12, 28, 31; 5:11, 13; 6:1, 18), suggesting that he has not completely written them off. And he seems to express some confidence that the Galatians will ultimately choose him over the agitators. As he says, "I am persuaded about you in the Lord that you will think no other thing" (Gal 5:10a). But was Paul's confidence ill-founded?

At the very least, the jury was still out at the time that Paul wrote Galatians. This is noticeably different from how Paul felt when he addressed the Thessalonians in his first letter to them.[2] As Paul narrates, he was waiting in Athens and sent Timothy to check in and make sure that they did not give up in the midst of the persecution they experienced after they received Paul's message (1 Thess 3:1–5). Because

2. For a fuller treatment of this, see Dunne, "Eschatological Emphases."

he wrote 1 Thessalonians *after he heard a positive word from Timothy*, as he recalls in 1 Thess 3:6–10, Paul does not have to express any ongoing concern or fear for them. But if 1 Thessalonians had been written while he was waiting to hear back from Timothy, it may have been a very different letter. First Thessalonians as it stands is focused on the imminent return of Christ; Jesus is again and again viewed as the one who will return. But if Paul wrote 1 Thessalonians while he was still waiting in Athens *before he heard back from Timothy*, I would imagine that the focus would have been different. Given their state of suffering, Paul likely would have incorporated more images of Jesus's death and crucifixion out of solidarity with their experience. By contrast, Galatians lacks the images of Jesus's imminent return, and instead focuses on the cross and speaks of Jesus mostly in terms of being crucified. That christological nuance between the two letters is rather suggestive to me, and it highlights how even something like Paul's Christology is occasioned by the situations that he is addressing. This is the case not because his Christology changes, but because certain emphases are needed pastorally. The Galatians needed an emphasis on the cross because their predicament of enduring hardship could lead them to give in or give up.

But this does not mean that the letter to the Galatians is any less concerned with the imminent transition into the age to come than we see in 1 Thessalonians. It is often said that Galatians lacks the same orientation towards the future that we see in 1 Thessalonians, but although the focus on the return of Christ is missing, imminent futurism is not, and this is important to acknowledge when we ask what Paul thinks might happen next.

Futurism in Galatians is clearly seen, for example, in the way that Paul talks about the Galatians in their situation of suffering. He asks them if it could all be in vain (Gal

3:4), which suggests that alleviating it would cause them to miss out on something, just as Paul worried that his gentile ministry (Gal 2:2) and even his specific Galatian ministry (Gal 4:11) could be in vain.

Paul also alludes to the final judgment on occasion. He calls the Galatians to "not grow weary while doing good, for in due time we will reap, if we do not give up" (Gal 6:9). "Not giving up" recalls how the Galatians need to endure and persevere in the light of that future day, which the harvest imagery clearly conveys. Paul also alludes to the final judgment when he says: his opponents will bear judgment (Gal 5:10), believers will bear their own load (Gal 6:5; cf. 6:17), people will boast about their own work (Gal 6:4; cf. 6:14), and those who receive circumcision in this conflict will have no future benefit from Christ (Gal 5:2). Justification itself, although Paul speaks of it as a present reality predicated on faith (Gal 2:16), anticipates the final judgment, which is why Paul speaks of awaiting "the hope of righteousness" (Gal 5:5). Those who will be vindicated are those who are destined to be "lord of all" (Gal 4:2), whereas those who are condemned will not inherit the kingdom of God (Gal 5:21; cf. 4:30).

Participating in this future, Paul says, is based on not giving up (Gal 6:9), and the "due time" for this future harvest when all of this occurs is near. Paul says that God sent his son in "the fullness of time" (Gal 4:4), which means that there is not much time left. When the metaphor of sons coming of age in Gal 4:1–7 is linked to this "fullness of time," the sons are now ready to receive their inheritance. Since the Spirit that the sons received is not the full inheritance, that must mean their inheritance ought to be coming very quickly, being that they are now of age and ready to receive it. Paul also alludes further to the lack of time in a few other places. He opens the letter by saying that Jesus "gave himself for our sins so that he might deliver us from the present evil age" (Gal 1:4), which suggests an imminent transition into the age to come. He also says "as we have time" we should do good to all (Gal 6:10), and he states that no one should cause him any further trouble "for the time that remains" (Gal 6:17). Indeed, the promised Spirit has been poured out, the new creation has started to emerge, and the regathering of Israel has begun; how much time could be left? The urgency for Paul is that there may not be much time before the Galatians make their move, and more importantly there may not be much time whatsoever.

WAS PAUL'S MINISTRY IN GALATIA A FAILURE?

We have to acknowledge that if the gentiles in Galatia did get circumcised, Paul would have viewed that as a failure. The whole letter was designed to ensure that they do not go down that path, and he reserves incredibly strong language for those who undergo the procedure in this context (cf. Gal 5:2–4). But receiving circumcision would not have meant, necessarily, that they themselves ceased to identify as followers of the Messiah. That would not matter much to Paul, but it would matter, sociologically at least, for the development of Christianity in Galatia. But it is not just that gentile circumcision would have been viewed as a failure for Paul. Getting circumcised in this context would have alleviated their social tension just as well as throwing in the towel altogether.

Robert Funk noted that Galatians is the only (undisputed) letter where Paul does not "anticipate a visit to the congregation in question."[3] The lack of any comment on an upcoming trip to check in on the Galatians is taken to suggest that Paul has already set his sights West at the end of

3. Funk, "Apostolic *Parousia*," 266.

his career and has no intention of returning to Asia Minor.[4] Yet it's just as likely that this could be explained by the fact that Galatians was written very early on in Paul's ministry before this became an established pattern for him. And it is also possible, as Funk himself notes, that the reference in Gal 4:20 of wanting "to be present with you now" in person to change his tone could communicate his desire for a return visit. Paul could have been inhibited from being there for any number of reasons, and maybe, fundamentally, Paul did not believe that there was much time before they made their fateful choice or before history itself came to an end.

J. Louis Martyn has suggested that Paul's ministry in Galatia was nearly an abject failure. Whatever the Galatians actually did, the vast majority of them did not listen to Paul.[5] Martyn bases this off of a couple of things related to Romans. To start, there is the observation that Romans does not mention that the Galatians contributed to the Jerusalem Collection, although Paul does say that Macedonia and Achaia did (Rom 15:26).[6] Additionally, Romans is an important clue for the non-success of Galatians for Martyn because, although Romans is similar to Galatians in some ways, it does not make all of the same points in exactly the same way.[7] It could be inferred from the differences that Paul adjusted his arguments by the time he wrote Romans because they did not work the first time. I argued earlier in chapter 1 that the differences between the letters are better understood in terms of the discrete occasions for which the two letters were written, but those who find Galatians to be a first draft to Romans, so to speak, have tended to view Paul as making necessary adjustments to his approach so as

4. Funk, "Apostolic *Parousia*," 266.
5. Martyn, *Galatians*, 29.
6. Martyn, *Galatians*, 227–28.
7. Cf., e.g., Martyn, *Galatians*, 350–52, 577.

to not make the same mistake twice. But is there any possibility that Paul's initial efforts in Galatia did end up being successful?

LITERARY EVIDENCE FOR THE SUCCESS OF PAUL'S GALATIAN MINISTRY

We sadly do not possess a letter entitled "Second Galatians," although that does not mean that Paul never wrote back to them. But there is other evidence in the NT where "Galatia" is referenced. These instances could provide us with some clues about how things fared after the Galatians read Paul's letter.

To start, there are references to Galatia in other Pauline letters like 1 Corinthians and 2 Timothy. As we saw in chapter 3, Paul writes near the end of 1 Corinthians about instructions for the collection for the saints:

> **1 Cor 16:1:** Now concerning the collection for the saints: just as I ordered the churches of Galatia, so also you should do.

If Galatians was written after 1 Corinthians, as most Pauline scholars argue, then this passage has no bearing on our question. But if Galatians precedes 1 Corinthians, this brief mention of Galatia could suggest a positive turn of events. I think it's significant that the instructions involve Paul's return visit to receive the collection (1 Cor 16:3), which makes it possible that Paul had already been back to Galatia by the time he wrote 1 Corinthians. This is admittedly dependent on too many factors, so I will just acknowledge that the mention of Galatia in 1 Cor 16:1 is of limited value unless you find it convincing that Galatians was written before 1 Corinthians and that Paul's silence about Galatia in Rom 15:26 need not be overstated.

Second Timothy likewise mentions Galatia a few times. In one instance it directly mentions "Galatia" by name, and then on the other occasion it refers to the cities of south Galatia mentioned in Acts 13–14. We will look at each in turn.

> **2 Tim 4:10–12:** For Demas deserted me, because he loved the present age, and he went to Thessalonica. Crescens went to Galatia, Titos went to Dalmatia. Luke alone is with me. Get Mark and bring him with you, for he is useful to me for service. And I sent Tychius to Ephesus.

Perhaps Crescens had a more amiable departure than Demas (though perhaps not), but regardless, why does he go to Galatia, and where exactly does he go? Since 2 Timothy was obviously written after Galatians (and most scholars would say it was written by a disciple of Paul after Paul died), this reference to Galatia could suggest an ongoing Christian presence there, though it is too brief to be considered good evidence of that.

The next 2 Timothy reference does not mention "Galatia," but it does refer to some Galatian cities:

> **2 Tim 3:10–12:** You followed my teaching, my conduct, my purpose, my faith, my patience, my love, my endurance, my persecutions, my sufferings, such as happened to me in Antioch, in Iconium, in Lystra, which persecutions I endured and the Lord rescued me from all of them. Now indeed all who want to live a godly life in Christ Jesus will be persecuted . . .

Here we read of the persecutions and sufferings that Paul experienced in Antioch, Iconium, and Lystra. Given the debate about authorship, part of the discussion here is whether Paul is recalling his experience, or if a later author knows the story from Acts or some other oral tradition about Paul's ministry. If Paul wrote this passage, then it highlights the indelible mark that these persecutions left on him (perhaps even literally). But this passage does not help us learn about what has transpired in those cities after Paul wrote Galatians. Although, if Crescens went to either Pisidian Antioch, Lystra, or Iconium when he went to "Galatia" (2 Tim 4:10), that would be significant, but that's not something we can know.

The evidence from Paul's letters, then, is fairly inconclusive, but there is evidence from another NT letter, namely, 1 Peter. The letter opens with the following:

> **1 Pet 1:1:** Peter, an apostle of Jesus Christ to the elect pilgrims of the diaspora of Pontus, Galatia, Cappadocia, Asia, and Bithynia.

We can perhaps guess that the Jesus followers of Galatia include many who originally heard the gospel from Paul. It may be worth noting that the pervasive emphasis on suffering and persecution in 1 Peter could reflect some of the conditions that began with the Galatian crisis, even though 1 Peter was written sometime later.[8] At the very least, it is noteworthy that another NT letter addressed to Galatia focuses so much on suffering and persecution. The fact that 1 Peter was written to Galatia could possibly suggest that some of Paul's converts remained loyal to Jesus (even if they did not remain so loyal to Paul).

The final bit of NT evidence comes from Acts. As we saw in chapter 3, after Paul went to the cities of south Galatia on his first missionary journey, he traveled back through Galatia on his second and third journeys. On the third journey, it reads:

---

8. On the topic in 1 Peter, see, e.g., T. Williams, *Persecution in 1 Peter*.

> **Acts 18:23:** After spending some time there he departed, passing through the Galatian and Phrygian region, strengthening all the disciples.

Strengthening disciples on Paul's third missionary journey suggests that he revisited churches and people that he already knew. If Galatians was written before the third missionary journey, then it would seem that things improved after the letter was sent. But this evidence is only convincing within a south Galatia framework and if Galatians is given an earlier date.

Outside of the NT there's one other text worth mentioning that could provide us with some clues about the endurance of the believers in Galatia. In the *Acts of Paul and Thecla*, which is a second century apocryphal text written very much in the style of the canonical book of Acts, we are given an origin story for the Cult of St. Thecla. The account takes place in Iconium, one of the cities of south Galatia in Acts 13–14 (cf. 2 Tim 3:11). It is not clear if the *Acts of Paul and Thecla* offers a revised version of what happened when Paul came to town, an independent report of that same visit, or a tale about a subsequent return visit after the narrative of the canonical book of Acts ends. Regardless, it is noteworthy that the *Acts of Paul and Thecla* records that the townspeople treated Paul with hostility as he taught his new disciple Thecla, and then that they also attempted to kill Thecla and make her a martyr after Paul left Iconium. They were unsuccessful, again and again, but the narrative highlights how this woman received Paul's message in south Galatia and underwent such extreme persecution. Even if the whole story is legendary, it would be notable that a legend like this emerged in Iconium, within the southern part of the province of Galatia, rather than in the north. Not only would such a legend further corroborate the idea that Paul and his converts were ill-treated in south Galatia, but it would suggest the ongoing Christian influence in the region, and the ongoing positive evaluation of Paul, after Galatians was written.

THE LEGACY OF GALATIANS

There are some good reasons to think that Galatians was successful to some degree (and this increases with an early date). But the letter's success should not only be measured in terms of whether the Galatians committed themselves to Paul's teaching. Success can also be measured by the letter's influence for generations as a canonical Christian text. This may have started with Paul retaining copies himself, or with the preservation of the letter by some of the Galatians who received it. Either way, it's endurance suggests something, even if such long-term influence was not something Paul could ever have imagined, not least because of his imminent expectation of the end. Perhaps if Paul knew his letter would become part of Christian Scripture, then he would have removed the bit about castration . . .

The success of Galatians can also be ascertained by the way it shaped the theological projects of prominent theologians and movements. Although not a great place to start, it was the heretic Marcion's favorite letter, judging by the fact that he placed it as first among the ten Pauline letters that he regarded as Scripture in his heavily edited and truncated canon. At the time of the Reformation, Galatians not only played a major role in the development of Martin Luther's theology, but Luther even called Galatians his "Katie von Bora," which intimated that Galatians was his favorite since he was married to Katie.[9] Galatians subsequently became centrally loved by Protestants, and because it was enshrined as one of F. C. Baur's four "Head Letters" (or *Hauptbriefe*),

9. Luther, *Lectures on Galatians 1535*, ix.

Galatians remained central in Protestant-dominated Pauline scholarship as well. Galatians helped to inspire the broader subdiscipline of rhetorical analysis, based on the initial work of Hans Dieter Betz. When the New Perspective on Paul was first beginning to develop, N. T. Wright recalls reading through Galatians with the insights of E. P. Sanders in mind and realizing that, "This whole thing is going to fly."[10] Conversely, the apocalyptic reading of Paul also found Galatians as its key resource, as demonstrated in the fact that the best articulation of this reading is J. Louis Martyn's commentary on Galatians. Galatians does not hold the same place of prominence in the Paul within Judaism crowd, however. That pride of place is probably given to Romans, or even to Acts, but Galatians does receive a lot of attention from this group because, as any Pauline interpreter would agree, Galatians creates the most interpretative challenges for their reading of Paul. But the way that Galatians has inspired so many different kinds of theological projects speaks to its generativity, if not ambiguity, and so it may very well be the biblical version of the Room of Requirement from *Harry Potter* after all. But its endless inspiration also confirms that regardless of what the initial readers of the letter did with it, it can only be regarded as a success in terms of its legacy, especially since we're all still trying to figure out what to do with it today.

REFLECTIONS

1. How significant would it be if Paul wrote a letter that did not accomplish what it set out to do?

10. Originally published as Tamerius, "An Interview"; this interview can be found online at http://hornes.org/theologia/travis-tamerius/interview-with-n-t-wright (accessed on May 22, 2024).

2. Why do you think Galatians has been so generative for different approaches to Pauline thought more broadly?

9

WHAT DO WE DO WITH PAUL'S LETTER TO THE GALATIANS?

TO ASK WHAT THE GALATIANS did with Paul's letter, as we did in chapter 8, is in one sense to ask how they "applied it to their lives," to borrow from Christianese. Given the fact that Galatians was later collected and canonized into Christian Scripture (which could in itself tell a story of Galatian perseverance), we must ask what relevance Galatians ought to have for subsequent generations of readers who are not faced with the same hostile situation of forced circumcision.

THE ORIGINAL APPLICATION OF GALATIANS

Of course, the original application of Galatians is straightforward: gentile men in Galatia should not be circumcised. That would have been clear to the original readers whether they complied or not. As I have tried to argue though, the issue of circumcision in the letter is not *circumcision per se*, but specifically *the forced circumcision* of gentile men.

Extrapolating from Galatians any kind of sweeping conclusion about circumcision for gentiles in other settings is unwarranted. Thus, Galatians cannot be used to say that the modern practice of circumcision in some parts of the West, especially in America, is invalid, where the default practice has largely been to circumcise baby boys, regardless of whether the family is Jewish (or, indeed, in spite of the fact that the vast majority of those families are not). There may be good reasons to oppose this practice, and presumably Paul would have done so if given the chance, but nevertheless Galatians itself is concerned with *forced circumcision*, not circumcision *per se*.

But doesn't all of this talk about circumcision just make Galatians a "guy thing," as Beverly Gaventa famously asked?[1] The short answer, in my view, is "No." There are a few reasons for this. First, circumcision itself was not simply a men's issue because, in that ancient culture, it was a household ritual long before it became an institutionalized ritual during the Rabbinic period. In the second temple period when Galatians was written, mothers would not only approve of the rite shortly after giving birth, but they may even have been the ones directly performing the rite to their sons (cf. Exod 4:24–26; 1 Macc 1:60–61; 2 Macc 6:10; 4 Macc 4:25).[2] So they still participated in the ritual even if they did not receive the procedure for themselves. But also, second, even though the Galatian crisis centers male genitals, it is noteworthy that Paul specifically de-centers them. He essentially says, on two different occasions, that it doesn't matter what someone's penis looks like (Gal 5:6; 6:15).

---

1. Gaventa, "Is Galatians Just A 'Guy Thing'?"

2. Blanton, "Did Jewish Women Circumcise Male Infants in Antiquity?"

Moreover, as Elisabeth Schüssler Fiorenza points out, Paul highlights the unity that arises from baptism for "males and females" in Christ (Gal 3:28). It is a ritual that has an equalizing force because, unlike circumcision, anyone regardless of gender can fully participate.[3] Not only that, but the baptismal formulation that "there is no *male and female*" does not stress the same binary as "there is no Jew nor Greek" and "there is no slave nor free." With "male and female" Paul does not speak to the gender binary, but rather their coupling. Given how circumcision was associated with marriage and procreation in that culture, it is noteworthy that baptism is not predicated on the coupling of "male and female" in the same way. Thus, beyond simply being inclusive of women, baptism as a ritual also relates to single people and couples without male children, or indeed any children at all, in a way that circumcision does not.

DERIVING PRINCIPLES FROM THE MAIN APPLICATION OF GALATIANS

Even though Galatians is about circumcision, and specifically forced circumcision, I think we can derive a number of principles from Galatians that are relevant to our lives today. To start, Galatians calls us all to be like Paul and to follow in his footsteps as he imitates and participates in the crucified Messiah. Just as Paul gives himself over to the realities of new creation, come what may, we need to share the same commitment to Christ and fidelity to the gospel. We aren't meant to go around looking for ways to suffer for Christ, but when those hardships do come, or if they've come already, Galatians is a resource for solidarity in the midst of turmoil.

---

3. Fiorenza, *In Memory of Her*, 205–41.

But what so often happens when Western Christians, especially those of us in America, hear about persecution in the early church, is that we tend to fold it into our own sense of being persecuted by broader culture. Even when the "persecution" we face is mostly benign and innocuous, or when our own brand of being obnoxious deservingly attracts admonishment, it still feeds our persecution complex. So rather than read Galatians by comparing our experiences to the persecution of Paul or the Galatians, which can perpetuate something amongst Western Christians that I want to curtail, we should be looking to the ways that we operate like the troublemakers, how we at times box people out from the community, and insist, even if implicitly, that people need get on board with our way of doing things.

Consider the old saying that Christians "don't drink, smoke, or chew, or go with girls who do." This suggests a particular approach to morality that casts aspersions on anyone who lives differently, even other Christians. The sentiment is that good Christians avoid, and then exclude others on the basis of, things like: watching R-rated movies, having tattoos, smoking cigarettes, drinking alcohol, voting Democrat, cussing and swearing, playing poker, concern about climate change, affirming evolution, vaccinations, wearing yoga pants, or—heaven forbid—reading *Harry Potter*. Christians today probably aren't forcing grown gentile men to be circumcised, but they might be barring entry or full participation in the community on the basis of things that Scripture does not address, and on the basis of things about which Spirit-led Christians may very well disagree.

THE GIFT OF THE SPIRIT

But beyond the issue of forced circumcision and whatever principles we can derive from it, the clearest application from Galatians, then and now, is that as Christians we ought to allow the Spirit to continually energize our lives.[4] Although the Spirit is not the full inheritance that we await as children of God, it is nevertheless a gift. The Spirit is received by faith, and so it is not earned in any way, which makes it an *unconditioned* gift. "Works of the law" were not a condition for receiving the Spirit, nor was anything else other than faith, which is a kind of self-denial and reliance on God.[5] But just because God's gifts are *unconditioned*, that does not mean, as John Barclay's study on gifts so rightfully demonstrates, that God's gifts are *unconditional*.[6] Once the gift is received, there are conditions for a gift-exchange to begin, not least the act of reciprocity to kick it off. To apply this to Galatians, the threat of apostasy and the call for the Galatians to endure speaks to those expectations of what ongoing life in the Spirit ought to be like: *beginning by the Spirit are you now perfected by the flesh* (Gal 3:3)? To undergo circumcision, after receiving God's gift, is a failure to appreciate the gift and amounts to rejecting it (cf. Gal 2:21). At the very least, it is not what God wants in return.

Gifts are typically generative; one gift begets another. Think about why two friends will go out for coffee and one of them will say, "I got you this time, you can get us next time." Why do we do that? Why not just have each person pay for themselves each time? The reason is to ensure that there is a next time. Gifts are meant to be reciprocated, and to further the development of the relationship.

---

4. The present section expands, summarizes, and adapts portions of a sermon that I have delivered in the past at Bethel University's chapel (September 13, 2019) and my home church, Mill City Church (November 14, 2021), called "The Spirit as Gift & Guide for Ordinary Time."

5. See Pifer, *Faith as Participation*.

6. Barclay, *Paul and the Gift*, 72–73, 446.

In the ancient world, this was more in keeping with how people normally understood gifts to function. Gifts were given to initiate and to maintain relationships, and so there was always an expectation of circularity. The notion of a "pure gift" that has "no strings attached" is actually a late development arising from the philosophy of Immanuel Kant (1724–1804).[7] But in the time of the NT, it was standard to offer a return gift after receiving one yourself.

Even today, let's not trick ourselves, we do not operate with a notion of gifts as having no strings attached to them, no matter what we might say. If an acquaintance at work gets you a gift for your birthday, you will likely feel bad for not recognizing their birthday, and then immediately try to figure out when it will roll around so that you can get them something. At Christmas time, when siblings get you gifts, don't you typically wonder what the value of the gift is so that you can get them something comparable in value? Or when you're invited to a wedding, the invitation doesn't say that you're only invited if you bring them a gift, but the registry is provided as a not-so-subtle reminder!

A brilliant illustration of this appears in the TV Show, *The Big Bang Theory*.[8] There's a wonderful sequence about gifts in the episode, "The Bath Item Gift Hypothesis" from Season 2. It originally aired in December 2008, and so it is set during the holiday season. The show is basically about a group of scientists, the main one being Sheldon (Jim Parsons), who live next door to a very attractive and down to earth woman named Penny (Kaley Cuoco) with whom they all struggle to relate. During this holiday episode, Penny incidentally mentions that she got Sheldon "a neighbor

7. See esp. Barclay, *Paul and the Gift*, 51–63.

8. I am grateful to Seth M. Ehorn for bringing this example to my attention in the context of Barclay's work on grace, which has greatly inspired how I address this topic.

gift." Sheldon reacts with some concern to this news. "Why would you do such a thing?" Sheldon asks to Penny's surprise. He goes on to explain, "I know you think you're being generous, but the foundation of gift-giving is reciprocity; you haven't given me a gift, you've given me an obligation." Penny quickly attempts to alleviate Sheldon's concern by stating, "you don't need to get me anything in return." "But, of course I do," Sheldon exclaims, "the essence of the custom is that I now have to go out and purchase for you a gift of commensurate value and representing the same perceived level of friendship as that represented by the gift you've given me."

Sheldon is clearly distraught by this news that Penny has a gift for him, but he conceives of "a fool-proof plan" to ensure that he does not over-, or under-, reciprocate. The plan is that he would go out and purchase multiple gift bags of varying value, and keep them tucked away in another room. Once Penny has revealed her gift to him, he would know precisely which gift bag was most comparable in value, and he would then give that gift bag to her. Then sometime later, having kept the receipts, he would return all the others "for a full refund."

So when it finally comes time to exchange gifts, Sheldon unwraps Penny's present to find . . . a napkin. He's a bit nonplussed at first, and he clearly doesn't know what to make of such a pedestrian gift. Then Penny tells him to turn the napkin over. And after doing so, Sheldon begins to lose his balance, clearly in shock at what's on the other side. It's a note, and it reads: "To Sheldon, Live long and Prosper—Leonard Nimoy." Of course, Leonard Nimoy is the actor who played Spock in the original run of *Star Trek*, a legendary icon of Sheldon's. Penny explains incidentally in a throw away manner, "He came into the restaurant; sorry the napkin's dirty, he wiped his mouth with it." At which point Sheldon abruptly returns to his feet, stumbling out of disbelief, visibly shaking, and staring incredulously at the napkin: "I possess the DNA of Leonard Nimoy?!" A thought suddenly occurs to Sheldon and he runs back into the room returning with *every single gift bag* that he had purchased. At the sight of this Penny shouts, "Sheldon! What did you do?" And Sheldon responds with, "I know . . . it's not enough, is it?" And then, rather unexpectedly and awkwardly, Sheldon moves in to give Penny a hug.

These scenes from this episode are wonderful for many reasons. Sheldon rightly articulates that a "no strings attached" approach to gift-giving is not in keeping with the origin of the custom, which is about reciprocity (as Barclay demonstrates so well). Sheldon's assumption, however, that gifts must always be symmetrical and proportional, and of the same relative value, is comically upended by his reaction to the *superabundant* gift that he received from Penny. In response, he gave all the gift bags that he had, and even threw in a hug to signify his immense appreciation for the great gift that he had received.

And so, what would giving gifts back to God look like in Galatians? It does not look like gentiles doing the law, because doing the law was not how the gentiles received the Spirit. But that does not mean that Paul was antinomian or anything like that. This is precisely because we give gifts back to God. But this is not a back door way to strive to earn God's gift. The gift of the Spirit simply cannot be earned, not least because as followers of Christ we already have it, and we have received it only by faith. Remember, gift-giving is about continuing a relationship that already exists, and so when we give gifts back to God it assumes that he has already given us his gift first. The gifts we give back to God are also not of the same kind that he gave us. God's gift to us of Godself is infinitely greater than the gifts we give back to God. In the gospel, the gift and the gift-giver are one and the same.[9] God gives us himself in the person of the Spirit, just as he gave himself in the person of his Son. Moreover, the gifts we give back to God are not of our own independent striving either because they are the outworking of God's gift in our lives, the fruit of the Spirit itself. Thus, the gifts given back to God in this gift exchange, so to speak, are part of the very gift that God gives to believers in the first place.

The shape of this is similar to how libations and offerings functioned in the OT temple system.[10] God provided the conditions to produce the crops and raise the livestock, and such agricultural production was recognized as God's ongoing gifts to Israel. Offering wine, grain, and other things back to God was to give from the gift he's already given. So with the production in our lives of the ninefold fruit of the Spirit, like a cluster of grapes, we offer back to God the libation of our very lives (cf. Phil 2:17; 2 Tim 4:6). Any good that we do, is the good that he works in us.

It all boils down to relying upon and trusting the Spirit, or, in Paul's words in Galatians, walking by the Spirit. As the Spirit animates our steps in response to the grace we have been given, we follow the rule of new creation and observe the law of the Messiah, bearing the burdens of others out of imitation of the one who loved us and gave himself for us.

REFLECTIONS

1. What are some ways that Christians can work at tearing down barriers to community?

---

9. Cf. Dunne and Williams, "A Perplexing Gift," 375–76.
10. See Dunne, *Mountains Shall Drip Sweet Wine*, chaps. 5–6.

2. How does recognizing the importance of reciprocity in gift-giving affect how we see our familial ties, friendships, and ultimately our relationship with God?

BIBLIOGRAPHY

Arnold, Clinton E. "Returning to the Domain of the Powers: *Stoicheia* as Evil Spirits in Galatians 4.3, 9." *Novum Testamentum* 38 (1996) 55–76.

Barclay, John M. G. "Mirror-Reading A Polemical Letter: Galatians as a Test Case." *Journal for the Study of the New Testament* 31 (1987) 73–93.

———. *Paul and the Gift*. Grand Rapids: Eerdmans, 2015.

Barr, James. "'Abbā Isn't 'Daddy.'" *Journal of Theological Studies* 39 (1988) 28–47.

Bekken, Per Jarle. *Paul's Negotiation of Abraham in Galatians 3 in the Jewish Context: The Galatian Converts—Lineal Descendants of Abraham and Heirs of the Promise*. Beihefte zur Zeitschrift für die neutestamentliche Wissenschaft 248. Berlin: de Gruyter, 2021.

Betz, Hans Dieter. *Galatians: A Commentary on Paul's Letter to the Churches in Galatia*. Hermeneia. Philadelphia: Fortress, 1979.

———. "Literary Composition and Function of Paul's Letter to the Galatians." *New Testament Studies* 21 (1975) 353–79.

Bird, Michael F. and John Anthony Dunne. "Pastoring with a Big Stick: Paul as Pastor in Galatians." In *Paul as Pastor*, edited by Brian S. Rosner et al., 71–82. London: T. & T. Clark Bloomsbury, 2017.

Blanton, Thomas R. "Did Jewish Women Circumcise Male Infants in Antiquity? A Reassessment of the Evidence." *Journal of the Jesus Movement in Its Jewish Setting* 10 (2023) 38–66.

Boakye, Andrew K. *Death and Life: Resurrection, Restoration, and Rectification in Paul's Letter to the Galatians*. Eugene, OR: Pickwick Publications, 2017.

Boccaccini, Gabriele. *Paul's Three Paths to Salvation*. Foreword by David Bentley Hart. Grand Rapids: Eerdmans, 2020.

Bowden, Hugh. *Mystery Cults of the Ancient World*. Princeton: Princeton University Press, 2010.

Brown, Jeannine K. *Scripture as Communication: Introducing Biblical Hermeneutics*. 2nd ed. Grand Rapids: Baker, 2021.

Buchanan, Grant. *The Spirit, New Creation, and Christian Identity in Galatians: Towards a Pneumatological Reading of Galatians 3:1—6:17*. Library of New Testament Studies 681. London: T. & T. Clark, 2023.

Campbell, Douglas A. *The Deliverance of God: An Apocalyptic Rereading of Justification in Paul*. Grand Rapids: Eerdmans, 2007.

———. *Framing Paul: An Epistolary Biography*. Grand Rapids: Eerdmans, 2014.

———. "Galatians 5.11: Evidence of an Early Law-observant Mission by Paul?" *New Testament Studies* 57 (2011) 325–47.

Collman, Ryan D. *The Apostle to the Foreskin: Circumcision in the Letters of Paul*. Beihefte zur Zeitschrift für die neutestamentliche Wissenschaft 259. Berlin: de Gruyter, 2023.

Cooley, Alison E. *Res Gestae Divi Augusti: Text, Translation, and Commentary*. Cambridge: Cambridge University Press, 2009.

Davies, W. D. *Paul and Rabbinic Judaism: Some Rabbinic Elements in Pauline Theology*. London: SPCK, 1967.

Davis, Basil S. "The Meaning of ΠΡΟΕΓΡΑΦΗ in the Context of Galatians 3.1." *New Testament Studies* 45 (1999) 194–212.

de Boer, Martinus C. *Galatians: A Commentary*. New Testament Library. Louisville: Westminster John Knox, 2011.

DeMaris, Richard E. "Water Ritual." In *The Oxford Handbook of Early Christian Ritual*, edited by Risto Uro et al., 391–408. Oxford: Oxford University Press, 2018.

Dibley, Genevive. "The Making and Unmaking of Jews in Second Century BCE Narratives and the Implication for Interpreting Paul." In *Israel and the Nations: Paul's Gospel in the Context of Jewish Expectation*, edited by František Ábel, 3–23. Minneapolis: Fortress, 2021.

Dunn, James D. G. *The New Perspective on Paul*. Grand Rapids: Eerdmans, 2007.

Dunne, John Anthony. "Cast Out the Aggressive Agitators (Gl 4:29–30): Suffering, Identity, and the Ethics of Expulsion in Paul's Mission to the Galatians." In *Sensitivity to Outsiders: Exploring the Dynamic Relationship Between Mission and Ethics in the New Testament and Early Christianity*, edited by Jacobus (Kobus) Kok et al., 246–69. Wissenschaftliche Untersuchungen zum Neuen Testament 2/364. Tübingen: Mohr Siebeck, 2014.

———. "Eschatological Emphases in 1 Thessalonians and Galatians: Distinct Argumentative Strategies Related to External Conflict and Audience Response." *Journal of Biblical & Theological Studies* 3 (2018) 227–48.

———. *The Mountains Shall Drip Sweet Wine: A Biblical Theology of Alcohol*. Biblical Theology for Life. Grand Rapids: Zondervan Academic, 2025.

———. *Persecution and Participation in Galatians*. Wissenschaftliche Untersuchungen zum Neuen Testament 2/454. Tübingen: Mohr Siebeck, 2017.

———. "Suffering and Covenantal Hope in Galatians: A Critique of the 'Apocalyptic Reading' and Its Proponents." *Scottish Journal of Theology* 68 (2015) 1–15.

———. "Suffering in Vain: A Study of the Interpretation of ΠΑΣΧΩ in Galatians 3.4." *Journal for the Study of the New Testament* 36 (2013) 3–16.

———. "'They Do not Keep the Law' (Galatians 6:13): Forceful Circumcision and the Fruit of the Spirit." In *Figuring the Enemy: Socio-Scientific and Biblical Approaches to Religious Enmity*, edited by Christopher A. Porter et al. Routledge Interdisciplinary Perspectives on Biblical Criticism. London: Routledge, forthcoming.

Dunne, John Anthony, and Logan Alexander Williams. "A Perplexing Gift: Towards Clarity in Evangelical and Mormon Interfaith Dialogues on Grace." *Journal of the Evangelical Theological Society* 60 (2017) 349–76.

Eastman, Susan G. "'Cast Out the Slave Woman and Her Son': The Dynamics of Exclusion and Inclusion in Galatians 4.30." *Journal for the Study of the New Testament* 28 (2006) 309–36.

———. "Israel and the Mercy of God: A Re-reading of Galatians 6.16 and Romans 9–11." *New Testament Studies* 56 (2010) 367–95.

———. *Recovering Paul's Mother Tongue: Language and Theology in Galatians*. Grand Rapids: Eerdmans, 2007.

Elder, Nicholas A. *Gospel Media: Reading, Writing, and Circulating Jesus Traditions*. Grand Rapids: Eerdmans, 2024.

———. "This Hand Is Validation: Philemon as a Pauline Holograph." *New Testament Studies* 70 (2024) 324–39.

Fiorenza, Elisabeth Schüssler. *In Memory of Her: A Feminist Theological Reconstruction of Christian Origins*. Tenth Anniversary Edition. New York: Crossroad, 1994.

Fredriksen, Paula. *Paul: The Pagans' Apostle*. New Haven: Yale University Press, 2017.

Bibliography

French, David. "Acts and the Roman Roads of Asia Minor." In *The Book of Acts in its Graeco-Roman Setting*, edited by David W. J. Gill and Conrad H. Gempf, 49–58. The Book of Acts in Its First Century Setting. Grand Rapids: Eerdmans, 1994.

Funk, Robert W. "The Apostolic *Parousia*: Form and Significance." In *Christian History and Interpretation: Studies Presented to John Knox*, edited by W. R. Farmer et al., 249–69. Cambridge: Cambridge University Press, 1967.

Gaston, Lloyd. *Paul and the Torah*. Vancouver: University of British Columbia Press, 1987.

Gaventa, Beverly Roberts. "Galatians 1 and 2: Autobiography as Paradigm." *Novum Testamentum* 28 (1986) 309–26.

———. "Is Galatians Just A 'Guy Thing'? A Theological Reflection." *Interpretation* 54 (2000) 267–78.

———. *Our Mother Saint Paul*. Louisville: Westminster John Knox, 2007.

Goddard, A. J., and Stephen Anthony Cummins. "Ill or Ill-Treated? Conflict and Persecution as the Context of Paul's Original Ministry in Galatia (Galatians 4.12–20)." *Journal for the Study of the New Testament* 52 (1993) 93–126.

Goodrich, John K. "Guardians, Not Taskmasters: The Cultural Resonances of Paul's Metaphor in Galatians 4.1–2." *Journal for the Study of the New Testament* 32 (2010) 251–84.

Gorman, Michael J. *Cruciformity: Paul's Narrative Spirituality of the Cross*. Grand Rapids: Eerdmans, 2001.

Hansen, G. Walter. "Galatia." In *The Book of Acts in its Graeco-Roman Setting*, edited by David W. J. Gill and Conrad H. Gempf, 377–96. The Book of Acts in its First Century Setting. Grand Rapids: Eerdmans, 1994.

Hardin, Justin K. *Galatians and the Imperial Cult*. Wissenschaftliche Untersuchungen zum Neuen Testament 2/237. Tübingen: Mohr Siebeck, 2008.

———. "Galatians 1–2 Without A Mirror: Reflections on Paul's Conflict with the Agitators." *Tyndale Bulletin* 65 (2014) 275–303.

Harmon, Matthew S. *She Must and Shall Go Free: Paul's Isaianic Gospel in Galatians*. Beihefte zur Zeitschrift für die neutestamentliche Wissenschaft 168. Berlin: de Gruyter, 2010.

Hays, Richard B. *Echoes of Scripture in the Letters of Paul*. New Haven: Yale University Press, 1989.

Heim, Erin M. *Adoption in Galatians and Romans: Contemporary Metaphor Theories and the Pauline Huiothesia Metaphors*. Biblical Interpretation Series 153. Leiden: Brill, 2017.

Heinsch, Ryan. *The Figure of Hagar in Ancient Judaism and Galatians.* Wissenschaftliche Untersuchungen zum Neuen Testament 2/579. Tübingen: Mohr Siebeck, 2022.

Hewitt, J. Thomas. "Πνεῦμα, Genealogical Descent and Things That Do not Exist According to Paul." *New Testament Studies* 68 (2022) 239–52.

Hodge, Caroline Johnson. *If Sons, Then Heirs: A Study of Kinship and Ethnicity in the Letters of Paul.* Oxford: Oxford University Press, 2007.

Hoehner, Harold W. "Did Paul Write Galatians?" In *History and Exegesis: New Testament Essays in Honor of E. Earle Ellis for His 80th Birthday*, edited by Sang-Won (Aaron) Son, 150–69. London: T. & T. Clark, 2006.

Hubing, Jeff. *Crucifixion and New Creation: The Strategic Purpose of Galatians 6.11–17.* Library of New Testament Studies 508. London: T. & T. Clark Bloomsbury, 2015.

Jerome, St. *Commentary on Galatians.* Translated by Andrew Cain. Fathers of the Church 121. Washington, DC: Catholic University of America Press, 2010.

Judd, Andrew. *Modern Genre Theory: An Introduction for Biblical Studies.* Studies in Method. Grand Rapids: Zondervan Academic, 2024.

Kahl, Brigette. *Galatians Re-Imagined: Reading with the Eyes of the Vanquished.* Paul in Critical Contexts. Minneapolis: Fortress, 2010.

Kennedy, George A. *New Testament Interpretation Through Rhetorical Criticism.* Studies in Religion. Chapel Hill: University of North Carolina Press, 1984.

Kern, Philip H. *Rhetoric and Galatians: Assessing an Approach to Paul's Epistle.* Society of New Testament Studies Monograph Series 101. Cambridge: Cambridge University Press, 1998.

Kim, Seon Yong. *Curse Motifs in Galatians.* Wissenschaftliche Untersuchungen zum Neuen Testament 2/531. Tübingen: Mohr Siebeck, 2020.

Kok, Jacobus (Kobus) and John Anthony Dunne. "Participation in Christ and Missional Dynamics in Galatians." In *Participation, Justification, and Conversion: Eastern Orthodox Interpretation of Paul and the Debate Between Old and New Perspectives on Paul*, edited by Athanasios Despotis, 59–85. Wissenschaftliche Untersuchungen zum Neuen Testament 2/442. Tübingen: Mohr Siebeck, 2017.

Landgraf, Paul David. "A Cinderella Story: The Role of Galatians within a Gospel Canon." In *Galatians as Examined by Diverse*

Academics in 2012 (St. Andrews, Scotland), edited by Heerak Christian Kim, 135–63. Newark, NJ: The Hermit Kingdom, 2013.

Levy, Ian Christopher. *The Letter to the Galatians*. Bible in Medieval Tradition. Grand Rapids: Eerdmans, 2011.

Longenecker, Richard N. *Galatians*. Word Biblical Commentary 41. Dallas: Word, 1990.

Luther, Martin. *Lectures on Galatians 1535: Chapter 1–4. Luther's Works* 26. Translated by Jaroslav Pelikan. St. Louis: Concordia, 1963.

Martyn, J. Louis. *Galatians: A New Translation with Introduction and Commentary*. Anchor Bible 33A. New York: Doubleday, 1997.

Matera, Frank J. "The Culmination of Paul's Argument to the Galatians: Gal 5:1—6:17." *Journal for the Study of the New Testament* 32 (1988) 79–91.

Meeks, Wayne A. *The First Urban Christians: The Social World of the Apostle Paul*. 2nd ed. New Haven: Yale University Press, 2003 [1983].

Mitchell, Stephen. *Anatolia: Land, Men, and Gods in Asia Minor*. 2 vols. Oxford: Clarendon, 1995.

Mitchell, Stephen, and Marc Waelkens. *Pisidian Antioch: The Site and Its Monuments*. London: Duckworth, 1998.

Nanos, Mark D. *The Irony of Galatians: Paul's Letter in First-Century Context*. Minneapolis: Fortress, 2002.

Novenson, Matthew V. "Our Apostles, Ourselves." In *Paul, Then and Now*, 1–12. Grand Rapids: Eerdmans, 2022.

———. "Paul's Former Occupation in *Ioudaismos*." In *Galatians and Christian Theology: Justification, the Gospel, and Ethics in Paul's Letter*, edited by Mark W. Elliott et al., 24–39. Grand Rapids: Baker, 2014.

Peterson, Eugene H. *Traveling Light: Galatians and the Free Life in Christ*. Foreword by Karen Swallow Prior. Downers Grove, IL: InterVarsity, 2023.

Pifer, Jeanette Hagen. *Faith As Participation: An Exegetical Study of Some Key Pauline Texts*. Wissenschaftliche Untersuchungen zum Neuen Testament 2/486. Tübingen: Mohr Siebeck, 2019.

Pobee, John S. *Persecution and Martyrdom in the Theology of Paul*. Journal for the Study of the New Testament Supplement Series 6. Sheffield: JSOT Press, 1985.

Ramsay, William M. *Historical Commentary on Galatians*. Edited by Mark Wilson. Grand Rapids: Kregel, 1997 [1900].

Richards, E. Randolph. *Paul and First-Century Letter-Writing: Secretaries, Composition and Collection*. Downers Grove, IL: InterVarsity, 2004.

Riches, John. *Galatians Through the Centuries*. Blackwell Bible Commentaries. Hoboken, NJ: Wiley-Blackwell, 2012.

Sanders, E. P. *Paul and Palestinian Judaism*. Philadelphia: Fortress, 1977.

Scott, James M. *The Apocalyptic Letter to the Galatians: Paul and the Enochic Heritage*. Minneapolis: Fortress, 2021.

Silva, Moisés. *Interpreting Galatians: Explorations in Exegetical Method*. 2nd ed. Grand Rapids: Baker, 2001.

Song, Kris. *One Spirit: Pneumatology and Unity in the Corinthian Letters*. Waco: Baylor University Press, 2024.

Soon, Isaac T. "The Bestial Glans: Gentile Christ Followers and the Monstrous Nudity of Ancient Circumcision." *Journal for the Jesus Movement in its Jewish Setting* 8 (2021) 116–30.

———. *A Disabled Apostle: Impairment & Disability in the Letters of Paul*. Oxford: Oxford University Press, 2023.

Staples, Jason A. *The Idea of Israel in Second Temple Judaism: A New Theory of People, Exile, and Israelite Identity*. Cambridge: Cambridge University Press, 2021.

———. *Paul and the Resurrection of Israel: Jews, Former Gentiles, Israelites*. Cambridge: Cambridge University Press, 2024.

Starling, David I. *Not My People: Gentiles as Exiles in Pauline Hermeneutics*. Beihefte zur Zeitschrift für die neutestamentliche Wissenschaft 184. Berlin: De Gruyter, 2011.

Stendahl, Krister. *Paul among Jews and Gentiles and Other Essays*. Philadelphia: Fortress, 1976.

Tamerius, Travis. "An Interview with N. T. Wright." *Reformation and Revival Journal* 11.1–2 (2003). http://hornes.org/theologia/travis-tamerius/interview-with-n-t-wright.

Thiessen, Matthew. *A Jewish Paul: The Messiah's Herald to the Gentiles*. Grand Rapids: Baker, 2023.

Weima, Jeffrey A. D. *Paul the Ancient Letter Writer: An Introduction to Epistolary Analysis*. Grand Rapids: Baker, 2016.

Williams, Jarvis J. *The Spirit, Ethics, and Eternal Life: Paul's Vision for the Christian Life in Galatians*. Downers Grove, IL: InterVarsity, 2023.

Williams, Logan. "Being(s) Above the Law: Ontology, Legislation, and Paul's Quotation of Aristotle's Politics in Galatians." Presented on November 20, 2022, at the 2022 Annual SBL Meeting in Denver, Colorado.

———. "Disjunction in Paul: Apocalyptic or Christomorphic? Comparing the *Apocalypse of Weeks* with Galatians." *New Testament Studies* 64 (2017) 64–80.

Williams, Travis B. *Persecution in 1 Peter: Differentiating and Contextualizing Early Christian Suffering.* Novum Testamentum Supplement Series 145. Leiden: Brill, 2012.

Wilson, Mark. *Biblical Turkey: A Guide to the Jewish and Christian Sites of Asia Minor.* Istanbul: Ege Yayinlari, 2010.

Wilson, Todd. *The Curse of the Law and the Crisis in Galatia: Reassessing the Purpose of Galatians.* Wissenschaftliche Untersuchungen zum Neuen Testament 2/225. Tübingen: Mohr Siebeck, 2017.

Winter, Bruce. "The Imperial Cult and Early Christians in Pisidian Antioch (Acts XIII 13–50 and Gal VI 11–18)." In *Actes du 1er Congres International sur Antioche de Pisidie*, edited by T. Drew-Bear et al., 65–75. Paris: Boccard, 2002.

Wright, N. T. *Justification: God's Plan & Paul's Vision.* Downers Grove, IL: InterVarsity, 2009.

———. *The New Testament for Everyone.* 3rd ed. Grand Rapids: Zondervan, 2023.

Yuh, Jason. "Analysing Paul's Reference to Baptism in Galatians 3.27 through Studies of Memory, Embodiment and Ritual." *Journal for the Study of the New Testament* 41 (2019) 478–500.

NAME INDEX

Ambrosiaster, 20, 114
Aquinas, Thomas, 20
Arnold, Clinton E., 101
Augustine, St., 20

Barclay, John M. G., 62–63, 142–43, 145
Barr, James, 102
Barth, Karl, 34
Baur, F. C., 10, 135
Bekken, Per Jarle, 96
Betz, Hans Dieter, 8, 12, 136
Bird, Michael F., 9
Blanton, Thomas R., 139
Boakye, Andrew K., 109
Boccaccini, Gabriele, 30
Bowden, Hugh, 70
Brown, Jeannine K., 47
Buchanan, Grant, 108
Bultmann, Rudolf, 14

Campbell, Douglas A., 26, 55, 119
Chrysostom, John, 20
Collman, Ryan D., 115
Cooley, Alison E., 72–73
Cummins, Stephen Anthony, 41

Davies, W. D., 23
Davis, Basil S., 44
de Boer, Martinus C., 26
DeMaris, Richard E., 52
Dibley, Genevive, 35
Dunn, James D. G., 24–25
Dunne, John Anthony, 9, 34, 42, 67, 104, 106, 119, 126, 146

Eastman, Susan G., 26, 106, 122
Elder, Nicholas, A., 6–7
Ehorn, Seth, 143

Fredriksen, Paula, 28, 29, 70, 98
French, David, 54
Funk, Robert W., 129–30

Gaston, Lloyd, 28, 30
Gaventa, Beverly Roberts, 26, 85, 139
Goddard, A. J., 41
Goodrich, John K., 100
Gorman, Michael J., 93

Name Index

Hansen, G. Walter, 54
Hardin, Justin K., 27–28, 63, 73
Harmon, Matthew S., 88
Hays, Richard B., 104
Heim, Erin M., 100
Heinsch, Ryan, 105
Hewitt, J. Thomas, 101
Hodge, Caroline Johnson, 28, 30, 101
Hoehner, Harold W., 11
Hubing, Jeff, 6

Jerome, St., 20, 73–74
Judd, Andrew, 5

Kahl, Brigette, 27–28
Kant, Immanuel, 143
Kennedy, George A., 12
Kern, Philip H., 12
Kim, Seon Yong, 106
Kok, Jacobus (Kobus), 42

Landgraf, Paul David, 10
Levy, Ian Christopher, 19–21, 31, 33
Longenecker, Richard N., 12, 53, 59
Luther, Martin, 22–24, 135

Marcion, 33, 135
Martyn, J. Louis, 25, 130, 136
Matera, Frank J., 14
Meeks, Wayne A., 125
Mitchell, Stephen, 54, 72

Nanos, Mark D., 4, 28
Novenson, Matthew V., 29, 46

Peterson, Eugene H., 1
Pifer, Jeanette Hagen, 142
Pobee, John S., 59

Ramsay, William M., 55
Richards, E. Randolph, 2
Riches, John, 19

Sanders, E. P., 23–25, 32, 136
Schüssler Fiorenza, Elisabeth, 140
Scott, James M., 34, 36
Silva, Moisés, 58
Song, Kris, 101
Soon, Isaac T., 70
Staples, Jason A., 109–10, 121
Starling, David I., 122
Stendahl, Krister, 23

Tamerius, Travis, 136
Thiessen, Matthew, 6, 28–30, 115

Victorinus, Marius, 20

Waelkens, Marc, 72
Weima, Jeffrey A. D., 2
Williams, Jarvis, J., 108
Williams, Logan, 33, 111, 146
Williams, Travis B., 133
Wilson, Mark, 72
Wilson, Todd, 113
Winter, Bruce, 27
Wright, N. T., 24–25, 33, 98–99, 103, 136

Yuh, Jason, 51

SUBJECT INDEX

Abraham, 2, 6, 26, 30, 33, 51, 77–78, 84, 94, 96–107, 121–22
agitators, 61–62, 64–71, 73, 75–81, 84, 106, 118–21, 123–26, 128, 141
alcohol, xi, 15, 47, 79, 141, 146
apocalyptic (interpretation), 19, 25–26, 32–34, 46, 95, 123, 136

baptism, 50–52, 60, 99, 113, 119, 140
The Big Bang Theory (show), 143–45

circumcision, 11–13, 16–17, 19, 22–23, 25–30, 32, 34–35, 39, 65–74, 76–81, 84, 89–90, 92, 95–96, 99, 103, 106–7, 110, 115–16, 118–22, 124–25, 128–29, 138–42
counter-imperial (readings), 19, 27–28, 34–35, 72–74, 81, 123

covenant, 24, 29–30, 32, 95, 123
cross/crucifixion, 26, 41, 43–45, 60, 67–71, 76, 92–93, 97, 105, 112, 115–16, 118–21, 124, 127, 140
Cybele, 70

Dan Gilbert's Open Letter, 63–64

faith, xii, 2, 4–5, 21–23, 25, 31, 43, 45, 50, 66, 91–93, 96–97, 99, 101–2, 109–12, 114, 120–21, 123, 128, 142, 145
Family Guy (show), 15
flesh, 41, 43, 47, 66–67, 69, 78–80, 102, 104–7, 110–11, 114–16, 119, 124, 142
freedom, 1, 51, 79, 89, 104–7, 114, 140
fruit of the Spirit, 1, 6, 15–16, 47, 106, 110–12, 114, 116–17, 119–20, 146

Subject Index

Galatia (North v. South), 43, 52–55, 58–59, 71–73, 88, 90, 131–35
Game of Thrones (novels/show), 98
grace, 21–24, 32, 92, 141–46

Harry Potter (novels/films), xi, 1, 136, 141
Independence Day (film), 48–49, 62

inheritance, 47, 60, 79, 96, 100, 102, 105, 106–7, 111, 128, 142

justification, 1–2, 21–23, 26, 31, 58, 90–93, 95–97, 99, 109–10, 114, 117, 123, 128
Judaism (ancient), 21, 23–29, 32, 35–36, 39, 45–46, 69–70, 80, 94–95, 139
Judaism (Rabbinic), 139
judgment, 106, 116–18, 128

Kingdom of God, 47, 59–60, 79–80, 102, 106, 111, 128

law, 6, 15, 19, 21–26, 29–33, 35–36, 39, 43, 69, 74, 78–79, 84, 90–92, 94–101, 107–16, 119, 122–23, 125, 142, 145

letters (writing and circulation), 2–14, 17, 89, 125–27, 129–31, 135
Lutheran (interpretation), 18, 22, 26, 31, 123

mirror reading, 62–64, 68, 75, 77–78, 80–81

New Perspective on Paul, 18, 23–25, 28, 32, 94, 123, 136

Patristic and Medieval (readings), 18–21, 30–31, 123
Paul within Judaism, 19, 28–30, 35, 39, 46, 95, 112, 123, 136
persecution, 5, 41, 43–46, 59–60, 66–69, 71, 74, 76–79, 81, 85–86, 92–93, 105–7, 118–19, 123–27, 129, 132–34, 138–41

relevance theory, 47–52, 60
rhetoric, 12–13, 136

suffering, 34, 38–45, 57–60, 66–68, 71, 78–79, 92–93, 105, 107, 127–28, 132–34, 140–41
Spirit, 13, 29–30, 36, 43, 45, 66–67, 69, 78, 84, 87–88, 95–97, 101–3, 105–17, 119–22, 124, 128–29, 141–43, 145–46

ANCIENT DOCUMENTS INDEX

HEBREW BIBLE / OLD TESTAMENT

Genesis — 104–5

1:14 LXX	101
15:6	96
17	78
17:12	29
21:9	105
21:10 LXX	106

Exodus

4:24–26	139

Leviticus — 109

18:5	110
18:5 LXX	109

Deuteronomy

25:4	6
27–32	97
27:26	97

Isaiah — 88, 104

49	87–88, 104
49:1–6 LXX	86
49:1 LXX	86
49:1b LXX	87
49:3 LXX	86–87
49:4a LXX	88
49:5 LXX	86
49:6	58, 86
49:6 LXX	86, 88
49:7 LXX	86
51:1–2	104
53	105
54	105
54:1	104
54:1 LXX	104

Jeremiah

1:5	87

Daniel — 25

Habakkuk — 109

2:4 LXX	109

OLD TESTAMENT APOCRYPHA

1 Maccabees

1:60–61	139

2 Maccabees

6:10	139

4 Maccabees

4:25	139

NEW TESTAMENT

Matthew

3:14	51
5:7	122

Mark

14:36	102

Luke

1:50	122
1:72	122

Acts 38, 52–53, 56–57, 59–60, 88, 133–34, 136

9–15	56
9:26–31	56
10–11	90
11	56
11:27–30	56
13–14	54, 56, 58–60, 71, 132
13:16–41	58
13:45	58
13:47	58, 88
13:50	58
14:2	58
14:3	58
14:5	58
14:6–7	58
14:8–18	58
14:19	59
14:22	54, 59–60
15	55–57
15:31	125
16	57
16:6	52, 54
18:2–3	8
18:23	52–54, 134

Romans 1–3, 7, 10, 130, 136

1:1	2
1:7	3
3:1–2	98
3:9–18	112
3:23	112
4:13–15	98
4:17	104
4:19	104
6	113
7	112
7:1–5	98, 111
7:1b	111
7:2–3	111
7:4	112
7:7–25	101
7:12	98
8:3–4	110
8:15–17	102
8:18–25	120
9:4–5	98
15:26	130–31

Ancient Documents Index

16:22	7	1:11–24	84–85
		1:11–12	75, 84

1 Corinthians 3, 10, 48–49, 131

1:1	2–3
1:2	4
1:10–17	51
5:6–13	106
7:17–24	123
9	6
9:9	6
9:19–23	123
10:18	121
16:1–4	48–49, 60
16:1	131
16:3	131

2 Corinthians 3, 10

1:1	2–3
4:4	5
5:17	120
11:25	59
12:1–10	40

Galatians

1–2	55–56, 84, 119
1:1–5	13
1:1	3, 75, 84
1:2	3, 49, 52, 84, 125–26
1:4	26, 120, 129
1:6–9	4, 13
1:6–7	61
1:6	4, 57–58
1:8–9	45, 60, 71, 106
1:10—2:21	5, 13
1:10–6:17	13
1:10	14, 76–77, 85–86, 88–89
1:11	46, 126
1:13–14	45, 60, 66, 86
1:13	41, 122
1:15–16	86–87, 118
1:15–16b	85
1:16c–17	X
1:18–19	56, 85
1:20	5, 56, 86
1:21	86
1:22–24	86
1:23	41
1:24	87
2	112
2:1–10	56, 84, 88–89
2:1	87
2:2	87, 128
2:2d	87
2:3–5	89
2:3	89, 93, 107
2:5	89, 115
2:6	89
2:7–9	89, 120
2:10–14	123
2:10	48–49, 55, 60, 89
2:11–21	85, 88, 90
2:12	70, 95
2:13	56
2:14	90, 93, 95, 107
2:15–21	36, 90, 112
2:15–17	90
2:15	92, 112
2:16	91, 95, 114, 128
2:18–20	92
2:18	112
2:19–20	44, 87, 112
2:19	92, 112
2:19a–b	109
2:19b	115
2:20	115
2:21	92, 142

(Galatians continued)

3	26, 32, 49, 101
3:1—6:10	13–14
3:1–5	38, 43–45, 58, 64, 66–67
3:1–3	43
3:1	5, 9, 43, 52, 60, 67, 79
3:2	66–67, 95, 102–3, 108
3:3–5	66
3:3	5, 66–67, 69, 107, 115, 142
3:4	66–67, 71, 107, 128
3:5	67, 95, 102, 108
3:6—4:7	33, 96
3:6–14	33, 96
3:6–9	33
3:6	96–97
3:7	96
3:8	96
3:9	96
3:10–14	109, 112
3:10–11	110
3:10	6, 97
3:11–12	109
3:13	97, 110
3:14	97, 110
3:14a	33
3:15–29	33, 96–97, 99–100
3:15–25	33, 99
3:15–18	6
3:15	126
3:16	6, 33, 97–99
3:17	97
3:19–25	98
3:19	100
3:21	108–10
3:21b	109
3:22	100
3:23	100
3:24–25	98
3:24	6
3:26–29	49–50, 60, 99, 113
3:26	99, 101
3:27–28	99
3:28–29	96
3:28	113, 140
3:29	99–100, 102, 121
4	78, 101, 103
4:1–7	33, 96, 99–100, 102, 128
4:1–2	100
4:2	102, 128
4:3–5	100
4:4	6, 101, 128
4:6	101–2
4:7	103
4:8–9	101, 115
4:10	28, 34, 101
4:11	103, 126, 128
4:12–20	38–39, 41, 44–45, 58, 64, 67, 103
4:12–15	39
4:12	14, 92, 126
4:13–15	39
4:13–14	44
4:13	40–42, 44, 57, 59–60, 65
4:14	40, 60
4:15–20	65
4:15	8, 39, 42
4:16–20	39
4:17	42, 65, 67, 71, 78–79
4:18	66
4:19	42, 52, 60, 93, 126
4:20	9, 126, 130
4:21—5:1	6, 96, 103
4:21	113, 125
4:23	104
4:26–27	122
4:26	104
4:27	104

4:28	103, 121, 126	6:8	110, 116
4:29	41, 78, 105	6:9	128
4:30	14, 105–7, 128	6:10	121, 129
4:31	104, 115, 121, 126	6:11–17	6, 8, 13, 110
5	15	6:11–18	13
5:1	14, 107, 115	6:11	6–7
5:2–6	11	6:12–16	11
5:2–4	35, 115, 129	6:12–13	68–69
5:2	128	6:12	31, 41, 73–74, 93
5:4	115	6:13	70, 118–19
5:5	114, 117, 128	6:14	26, 44, 118–19, 128
5:6	120, 139	6:15	26, 110, 119–20, 139
5:7–12	68	6:16	6, 121–22
5:9	106	6:17	6, 41, 44, 59, 92, 118, 128–29
5:10–12	71	6:18	6–7, 13, 126
5:10	106, 128		
5:10a	126		
5:11	41, 44, 76–77, 119, 126		

Ephesians 3, 10, 57

1:1	2–3

5:12	9, 106, 135		
5:13–14	114, 116		
5:13	79, 126		
5:14	79		
5:15	79		

Philippians 3, 10

1:1	2–4
2:17	146
2:27	122
3:5	29
3:6	5

5:16–17	115–16		
5:18	113, 117		
5:19–23	106		
5:19–21	xi, 45–46, 60, 79		
5:21	47, 102, 128		
5:22–25	117		
5:22–23	6, 110–11		

Colossians 3, 10

1:1	2–3
4:18	6

5:24	44, 112, 115
5:25	114
5:26	116
6:1	117, 126
6:2	116–17
6:3–5	118
6:4	128
6:5	117, 128
6:6	125
6:7–9	110, 116
6:8–9	117

1 Thessalonians 3, 10, 55, 126–27

1:1	3
2:4–5	76
2:9	7
3:1–5	126
3:6–10	127

2 Thessalonians   3, 10

1:1	3
3:7–8	7
3:17	6

1 Timothy   3, 10

1:1	2
1:2	122
1:15	5

2 Timothy   3, 10, 131–32

1:1	2
3:10–12	132
3:11	59
4:6	146
4:10–12	132
4:10	133

Titus   3, 10, 57

1:1	2

Philemon   3, 7, 10

1	3
4–5a	4
8–22	2
19	6–7

1 Peter   133

1:1	133

Revelation   25

NON-CANONICAL JEWISH WRITINGS

1 Enoch   25

Epistle of Enoch   34

4 Ezra   25

7:104–105	118

2 Baruch   25

Jubilees

15:25–26	29

Josephus

Against Apion

2.143	125

NEW TESTAMENT APOCRYPHA

Acts of Paul and Thecla   134

GRECO-ROMAN SOURCES

Aristotle

Politics

3:8 1284a   111

Plutarch

Cato Major

20:4–5 (348)   6

www.ingramcontent.com/pod-product-compliance
Lightning Source LLC
Chambersburg PA
CBHW030113170426
43198CB00009B/607